His Heart Revealed
Living With Secrets and Lies

By Jean Smythe

Copyright © 2012 by Wilma Smith

His Heart Revealed
Living with Secrets and Lies
by Wilma Smith

Printed in the United States of America

ISBN 9781625091239

All rights reserved solely by the author. The author guarantees all contents are original and do not infringe upon the legal rights of any other person or work. No part of this book may be reproduced in any form without the permission of the author. The views expressed in this book are not necessarily those of the publisher.

Unless otherwise indicated, Bible quotations are taken from The King James Version.

www.xulonpress.com

Table of Contents

Introduction vii

Chapter 1 15

Chapter 2 23

Chapter 3 35

Chapter 4 46

Chapter 5 59

Chapter 6 72

Chapter 7 87

Chapter 8 93

Chapter 9 100

Chapter 10 111

Chapter 11 186

Chapter 12 193

Chapter 13	200
Chapter 14	216
Chapter 15	239

INTRODUCTION

I did not hear the final gunshot, but in my heart and mind, I have heard it over and over, louder and louder each time, as it continues to echo across my years of struggle, heartache, and pain. In spite of reaching out for help to family, friends, our pastor, and even the police, there seemed to be no way out of the nightmare that had permeated our lives. My husband had become such a respected man in our community that my cries for help were never taken seriously.

I have had so many questions about this time in my life. Our life together was never easy, and I have always been haunted by the actions of this man and struggled with a great guilt over what my children and others suffered at his hands.

I did not understand the "why" of the abuse I endured throughout our married life. After a few years, it didn't seem to matter anymore. I had come to accept that there are things I was not meant to understand. I believed that there was purpose in my past, and that God would use it for his good. (Romans 8:28).

But God did intend for me to understand the "why." Twenty-five years after my husband's death, in a matter of seconds, and in God's perfect timing, He opened that door and the truth tumbled right into my lap. In John 8:32, Jesus said, "And ye shall know the truth, and the truth shall make you free." The truth did make me free, but it was not an easy path and one that was filled with a great deal of pain and agony.

Even now, I know there is much I do not know and that I can only imagine. I have probed

Introduction

Keith's mind and heart many times and have even considered the possibility that he had multiple personalities. Through all of this, I have learned that only God knows our hearts. He has provided all I needed to bring closure to that part of my life. And for that, I am so grateful.

The one thing I am sure of is that God never left me. There were many times that I felt alone and could not feel his presence, but I do know that without Jesus in my life, neither my children nor I would have survived the turbulence of those years. In the midst of it all, God was there. Sometimes He covered us with His hand; sometimes He surrounded us with angels. Sometimes I could only know His love from that still, small voice. Often I could not feel His presence, but I always knew that He was there. I have learned so many lessons throughout my life, but the greatest lesson has been that God loves me and will never leave me—no matter how great the trial.

Today, women have so many avenues to receive help when abuse prevails. As you read my story, remember that this part of my life occurred when resources and the support were not readily available, and the traditional mindset of the husband's role in a wife's life was much different than it is today. Even though I struggled through this relationship, I do not believe that God intends for us to live this way. I encourage women who are living with abuse to reach out for help and find the road that leads to a better life, the life God intends for you to live.

Most importantly, this is not a story about me but it is a story about God's promises. He is the same yesterday, today and tomorrow and will never leave us or forsake us. If you have never accepted Jesus Christ as your Lord and Savior, I encourage you to do so. Jesus paid the price for your sin and mine by giving His life on a cross at a place called Calvary. God brought Jesus back from the dead and provided the way

Introduction

for us to have a personal relationship with Him through Jesus. Sin grieves the heart of God and each one of us desperately needs a Savior. To admit we are sinners means turning away from our sin and selfishness and turning to follow Jesus. God's offer of salvation is open to you. It is a free gift and Jesus is holding this gift out for you right now. All you have to do is accept it.

9 That if thou shalt confess with thy mouth the Lord Jesus, and shalt believe in thine heart that God hath raised him from the dead, thou shalt be saved. 10 For with the heart man believeth unto righteousness; and with the mouth confession is made unto salvation.

Romans 10:9-10

ಬ್ಬಾಡ್

This story is dedicated to my children who have broken the cycle of generational sin and kept their focus on Jesus Christ. I would live through it all again just to have the three of you.

Chapter 1

ಸಂಞ

"And we know that all things work together for good to them that love God, to them who are the called according to *his* purpose."
Romans 8:28

I grew up in a family of seven with an older sister and brother and a younger sister and brother. My father worked as a telegrapher for the railroad. He was a gentle, quiet man who loved his family but avoided conflict no matter the cost. He spent many hours working and few hours interacting with us. I remember my mother as an angry woman most of the time;

in her later years she would be diagnosed with schizophrenia. Although my parents took us to church regularly and I grew up in the Word, our home life was far from "normal."

I gave my heart to Jesus Christ when I was nine years old. When I was sixteen, I felt God calling me into special service and publicly surrendered my life to His control. I just knew that God would call me to some exotic country, or he would send a handsome missionary for me to marry.

The summer between my freshman and sophomore year of college, I spent as a Volunteer in Service to America (VISTA volunteer) living in a poverty-stricken area. The following summer, I served as a summer missionary for the Southern Baptist Home Mission Board. I was actively searching for His plan for me, and my life seemed to be on track as I continued working on a degree in education.

Chapter 1

One Sunday evening it happened. It was one of those moments that, in retrospect, I wish I could have changed, but I can still vividly remember the magic of his charm. One of my best friends brought her cousin, Keith, to church. He was visiting from a town nearby. I was surprised to recognize him as a friend from my past.

When I first met Keith, he was a ten-year-old boy with a face full of freckles and dark, curly hair. My family had just moved to town. I started fifth grade at a new school, and Keith was one of my classmates. We attended the same schools through our sophomore year in high school and often had classes together. We were both raised in Christian homes, attended the same church, and were involved in many youth activities together. We became friends over those years.

At the end of my sophomore year, my dad was transferred, and my family packed up and moved again. I started a new school and became involved with a youth group at a local church. I was very active in this group, and my whole social life revolved around these Christian friends. This is the group that brought him back into my life. We had not seen each other in three years. He was happy-go-lucky and was the type of person that everybody enjoyed being around. He had such charisma, and everyone was drawn to his great sense of humor and charm.

We all went out after church that night and had so much fun. I was eighteen years old and just on the edge of adulthood. I had dated some since I was sixteen, but had never been as drawn to anyone as I was to Keith. He was different. He was thoughtful and attentive and so much fun to be around. He treated me as though I was someone to be valued. Coming from a dysfunctional home life, I found that to be magical.

In the weeks that followed, he and I were drawn together, enjoying one another's com-

Chapter 1

pany in such a comfortable way, that we soon became a twosome in the group. The more we saw of each other, the more I knew that he was the one I wanted to share my life.

Our relationship was everything I had always hoped to have. He was an incurable romantic, always polite and respectful and so much fun to be around. We did not argue or fight and always seemed to agree on everything. We liked the same songs and movies and enjoyed the same activities. He was always ready and willing to attend church services and activities. He would send me flowers and cards for no reason. His caring attitude and actions toward me always made me feel special, which was quite a change from my childhood.

We dated for two years when an incident occurred that caused me to question our relationship. I had never been around alcohol, so I was very naïve. We planned on going to the movies, but instead when he picked me up we skipped the movies and went out to eat. That night he begged me to elope with him. He was so adamant about his love for me and seemed so sincere. At first, I was thrilled that he wanted to marry me, but I knew something just didn't seem right. He was too desperate, and as time passed he began to slur his words. I finally realized that he was drunk and called a friend to pick me up.

The next day he came over, and we had a long conversation about drinking. He told me that he would always drink and that it would just have to be something that I accepted. I told him that I couldn't accept it and that, even though I loved him, I did not want alcohol to be a part of my life. We broke up that night, and I was heartbroken.

Keith got his pilot's license and completed his coursework for his airframe and power plant license (A & P). He joined the Army Reserves and went to basic training.

Chapter 1

College classes started up again. I moved in with a new roommate and in the move came across Keith's class ring. I boxed it up and mailed it back to him. Within a week I received a friendly letter from him. We continued to write newsy letters back and forth, and after four months he wrote me and told me that he had two week's leave at Christmas and wanted to see me when he came home. The magic happened all over again, and we picked up where our relationship ended six months earlier.

We spent Christmas Eve together and it was after dinner that he asked me to marry him. My answer was a definite yes. I want to think that he truly loved me in the beginning, but I wonder if I was simply the "good Christian girl" that he always thought he should marry. I tried very hard to live a life that followed biblical values and later learned that he had lived a life of sex and parties. I had experienced so little love in my childhood, and I was so hungry to be loved. He was kind and attentive to me, and I felt like I was the most special person in his life. Unfortunately I had no idea how much this decision would change the direction of my life. Looking back, I know that God gave me a warning when we broke up, and I eventually chose to ignore it. This decision was the greatest turning point of my life and one that not only affected my life, but deeply affected the lives of my children as well.

Chapter 2

ℰℴℛ
"The LORD *is* my strength and my shield; my heart trusted in him, and I am helped: therefore my heart greatly rejoiceth; and with my song will I praise him."
Psalms 28:7

We married in the spring. I thought I had found my "prince" and knew we would live "happily ever after." I promised to "love and obey, in sickness and in health, till death do us part." I was not just following tradition, but I was sincerely making a commitment as I stood before God and Keith. I did not realize the full extent of that commitment.

We moved 200 miles away from our families and rented a small apartment. Our life as husband and wife began. Keith worked as an airplane mechanic, and I took a job as a secretary. We spent the next few months getting to know one another, and I thought we were constructing the framework that our relationship would be built upon.

Our life together was calm. Keith, who had never drank in front of me, began to drink every night at home. Although I worried about it, he seemed to be able to keep things together. I began to accept it as a part of who he was.

After five months of marriage, Keith decided that he wanted to make a career change and go back to college. We moved back to our home town and enrolled in school. We both worked full time, and Keith started classes. He continued to drink, and there were times that I felt that his drinking was not always in his control. The quantity of alcohol he consumed in front of me

Chapter 2

had increased considerably since the day we said "I do." I still convinced myself that he was fine. I just knew that I could not have been mistaken about the wonderful life we would have together. I never once suspected the battle with which he was already struggling.

I became pregnant during our second year of marriage. This baby was something that we both wanted, and we were thrilled. By this time, Keith was drinking at least two six-packs of beer a day and kept a bottle of scotch around the house. Whenever I mentioned my concern, he would fly into a rage.

I was not very sympathetic or compassionate about his drinking and still more than a little pious when I brought the subject up. I did not realize that he was already addicted to alcohol nor did I understand he drank to block out the sins of his youth that had begun to cry out to him. Satan had his stronghold, and marriage alone did not break those bonds.

During my sixth month of pregnancy, an incident occurred that marked the beginning of the horror that was to come. It was a cold, wintery evening and already dark when I arrived home from work. Keith's pickup sat in front of the house so I knew he was already home. When I entered the room I found him hunched down in his chair with his .357 Magnum pistol in his lap. One look at him and I realized he probably had come home from work very early in the day. I could see that he had been drinking for hours. His face was red and his eyes already had that glazed over look. Beer cans were scattered around the room, and on the floor next to his chair lay an almost-empty bottle of scotch. His eyes had a wild look, and he was shaking. I knew our evening would be hard, but I had no idea that my life was about to be turned upside down.

We had just moved into our little house in the country and still did not have a phone. We had

Chapter 2

---

no close neighbors, and with no phone, I knew that I could not call for help. (This was before cell phones and the Internet, so we were very isolated.) When I realized what was happening, I immediately turned back towards the door thinking I would go for help. He cocked the pistol and pointed it towards me and told me to stop.

For just a second, I felt the unreality of the situation swirl around me. He stood up, still clutching the pistol, and stumbled towards me. I felt a fear rise up in me which was so intense it would have been impossible to imagine that, in years to come, this would become a normal, recurring emotion. I reached for the door knob as he grabbed me and slammed me into the door. He shoved the pistol barrel against my head. I still remember the hard coldness of the pistol as he held it against my temple. "I'm going to kill you," he mumbled as he pushed me harder into the door.

I stood there paralyzed. "Oh, please God," I cried out as I shut my eyes tight and wrapped my arms around my stomach hoping to protect my baby. "Please help us." My mind was spinning trying to absorb what was happening. He was quiet for a minute then he pulled the gun away and pushed me to the floor. He laughed, turned, and stumbled back to his chair, grabbed the bottle of scotch and took a big drink.

I was groping for some semblance of sanity, but my thoughts were jumbled as I tried to decide what I should do. If I could get away, should I call the police or my family or his family? How could I betray my husband by calling for help? I stood up and moved slowly to the sofa. Maybe if I just remained calm everything would change. I picked up my purse and coat from the floor and threw them on the sofa.

"Put the gun down, Keith," I said. "Please put the gun down. You have had too much to drink.

Chapter 2

You don't really want to do this." I repeated myself, "Just put the gun down."

"No, I haven't had too much to drink. You are the problem. You are the one who has caused all of my problems." He continued shouting obscenities but his words became so slurred I couldn't make sense of what he was saying.

He took the last drink from his bottle and threw it across the room. The bottle seemed to float in the air in slow motion until it hit the wall and shattered. Suddenly, picking up the broken glass brought reality to the situation. It gave me something to do, an action to take. I moved across the room towards the mess. "Get me another bottle," he yelled.

"I think you've had enough," I said. "I'll fix supper. You will feel better if you eat."

He raised the gun to his head and stuck the barrel into his open mouth. I froze in horror. Time seemed to stop. Surely, I was dreaming. As the seconds ticked away, he removed the gun and once again pointed it at me. He stood up and moved over to my side.

He slammed me down on the floor and again placed the gun to my head. Suddenly he moved the gun from my head to my protruding stomach. "I'll just kill us all," he said. How could he do this, I wondered? How could he threaten to destroy this child that had already brought so much joy into our lives? I had no idea what I was supposed to do or say next. I knew I could not overpower him and I also knew that when he was like this he was capable of killing both of us.

This realization came to me like a fist in my gut. We had only been married two years, and I had known for a long time that something was wrong. But I just kept pretending that our marriage was strong and that I had a wonderful husband. All I could do now was to try to keep him calm and pray that he would either pass out or come to his senses and that we would all somehow survive the night. Isaiah 26:3 had

Chapter 2

---

been the focus of my Bible study that morning. It ran through my mind. I cried it out to God, "I trust you to be in control of my life. Give me Your peace even in the middle of this chaos. Take my fear."

The horror of that moment was overwhelming and the fear I felt had become a physical pain. For six more hours he played with the gun, holding it to his head, to my head, and to my stomach. He cursed me. He ranted and raved, spewing vulgarities that filled the night with such an ugly darkness. I feared that if I argued or fought back, he would kill one or all of us. He drank until there was nothing left in the house to drink. I kept quiet and continued to cry out to God for His mercy.

Finally, Keith staggered to the kitchen, looking for another bottle. My chance had come. As he walked past me I reached out and grabbed the gun and wrestled with him. It was early morning, and the alcohol had finally slowed his reflexes.

His Heart Revealed

He lost his balance, and I felt the gun slip from his grasp as he fell.

His fall gave me the time I needed. I ran outside into the middle of the field behind our house and threw the gun as far as I could. Then I ran behind a small storage building and crouched down. He raced out the door, searching for me. He was crazy, screaming things I couldn't quite hear or understand. When he could not find the gun or me, he got into his pickup and drove away. I watched him go, seeing the shadow of the rifle hanging on the mounted rack in the back window of the pickup.

I was glad that he was gone but it was at that very moment that I realized how alone I was. There was nowhere I could go. There was no one I could call to help me without betraying my husband. His family would never have believed me, and I knew that my father would not interfere no matter how serious the charge. I was twenty-three years old, pregnant, and alone and had

Chapter 2

just been introduced to the nightmare that would become my life for the next fourteen years.

Just before the sun came up, he returned home and went to bed. The pickup had a bullet hole in the roof. At the age of twenty-four, he had made his first suicide attempt.

As I was getting ready for work the next morning, he came into the front room. He acted as if nothing had happened and was relaxed and happy. He did not seem to have a hangover. When I confronted him about his insane actions, he looked at me in confusion. I was in such turmoil, and yet the feeling of disbelief still persisted. I don't know how long I stood there as I realized that he did not remember the night before. An overwhelming fear engulfed me. Was I the one that was crazy?

But then his attitude changed and he apologized. This was the first of many apologies and promises that would come my way over the years. If I had known the truth of what caused this incident, I probably would have tried to leave him then. Even this early in our marriage, I don't think I could have left without risking my life. But not understanding the reason for his actions, I just knew that I loved Keith so much and in my heart I knew that I had made a commitment, not only to Keith, but also to God and that extended to my child. I realized that I couldn't just think of myself anymore. I had a child that needed a loving home with two parents. Little did I know that would never be. I accepted the first of his weak responses and life resumed.

The horror of the moment began to fade quickly, and I began to think I had exaggerated the whole incident. I did not know that it would happen again and again and again. And the lesson that I had learned that night was that if I could just stay calm and not add to his anger, we would all somehow survive the night. The stage was set for what was to come.

Chapter 3

"But they that wait upon the LORD shall renew their strength; they shall mount up with wings as eagles; they shall run, and not be weary; and they shall walk, and not faint."
Isaiah 40:31

Two major events occurred in our lives. Keith graduated from college with his bachelor's degree and, more importantly, our daughter was born. For a short time Keith's whole focus of life changed with her birth. He seemed to be a proud father. He still drank and there were still those times that he would lose control, but for a short time he seemed content.

He accepted his first teaching job at a high school in another town. I was ready to move again, hoping that this would be a new beginning for everything. He loved teaching and was very successful. His students grew to love him and soon recognized and came to rely on his seemingly, sincere concern and involvement in their lives. I thought he had found his calling.

We joined a small church and, for the first time in our married lives, we became part of a church family. The minister had pastored our church back home when we were children. It was a blessing to be led by someone we knew, and he and his wife provided us much-needed fellowship and support. They made us feel loved and with their encouragement we stepped out and developed Christian friendships. I thought that our lives were headed toward the "happily ever after" that I had always dreamed about.

I do not know how sincere Keith was, but he seemed to be actively seeking change

Chapter 3

in his life. He made efforts to cut back on his drinking and actually talked about giving up alcohol all together. People in our church were so impressed with him. He was highly respected and was on the path to becoming a leader in the church.

But in just a few months Keith began to show signs of discontent. His drinking escalated again, worse even than it had been before. Almost overnight the man I had promised to love and obey was gone. From then on he was always either a "Dr. Jekyll or Mr. Hyde." Mr. Hyde was the dark side of Dr. Jekyll unleashed by the use of a potion, and I related that directly to the alcohol. There was no more doubt in my mind. I knew that my husband was an alcoholic.

During the day when he was at work, he was full of energy, productive, happy, and content. But almost as soon as the sun went down and he was home drinking, a new personality would emerge. He would fall into fits of depression and would cry and curse me and drink more. He would babble on and on making no sense. As the evenings wore on, he would become loud, violent, and aggressive. These episodes occurred three to four times a week, but, once again, I was thankful that he did not bring out any of his guns.

I believed that I was protecting our one-year-old daughter from his frequent outbursts. She would usually be in bed asleep when things escalated but now I realize that she was greatly affected by his behavior.

Through all of this, family and friends were not aware of our problems. It became our "family secret." I thought we were keeping the alcoholic problem a secret, but now I know he was keeping a bigger secret from all of us.

We lived in this town for less than a year when Keith's grandfather died. He owned a small acreage near our hometown, and we decided to buy the land and move. Keith was hired at

Chapter 3

a high school about thirty minutes away from our little farm. I was a stay-at-home mom, once again hoping that this move would be the new beginning for us. But I soon realized that with this move, just as with the others, we brought all of the "baggage" with us.

For a while Keith was able to keep some semblance of peace at home, but I knew that our lives had been forever changed. His "Dr. Jekyll and Mr. Hyde" behavior became the norm in our lives, although for a short time I saw more of his Dr. Jekyll side.

Change is constant in life, and it was time for more changes. I became pregnant with our second child. The newness had worn off Keith's job, and he was drinking heavily again. He seemed to be in constant stress and turmoil. So once again he decided it was time for a move. This time we didn't move far. We bought a house in town, and he continued teaching at the same high school. He picked up a weekend job driving a truck for a refinery. He was teaching during the day and often had meetings at night. On weekends he would be on the road. So for my daughter and I, there was peace and contentment when he was gone.

And then one quiet, unsuspecting Saturday evening the nightmare from two years earlier returned. Keith had left the evening before to carry a load of fuel up north, and I did not expect him back for two days. Our daughter, who was now two years old, was in bed and I had just gotten to sleep. I was awakened suddenly with a gun pressed against my head. My first thought was that someone had broken into our house, and I feared for my daughter's safety. But as I came more fully awake, I heard Keith's laughter, and with a sinking heart, I knew that it was happening again. It was three hours later before he finally passed out and I was able to get the pistol and leave the room.

Chapter 3

I hid the pistol and paced the floor for hours knowing that I could not live this way. I knew I had to reach out for help. I finally called my father even though it was in the early morning hours. I could tell I woke him up, but I was in such turmoil that I couldn't wait for daylight. I also knew that Keith would eventually wake up, and I did not have the strength to deal with him. As I talked with my father about my fears, he told me that he was sorry but he had given me to Keith many years ago. He could not interfere in my marriage. Even though I tried to explain that I felt I was in a life-and-death situation, he humored me, but I knew he did not believe what I was saying. He believed that divorce was not an option for any marriage.

I waited for the sun to come up, and then I called Keith's parents. I was desperate and decided that I had to find someone who would help us. I talked with them about his excessive drinking and told them about the incidents when he threatened to kill me. Even though they heard me out, they reminded me that Keith had to work long and hard hours and of course he would be stressed and worn out when he got home. They said that they understood that I was pregnant and with all the changes in my body, I probably was thinking that things were worse than what they were.

When Keith woke up, I was furious with him. I ranted and raved and screamed at him. I threatened to leave with our daughter. He went back to the bedroom and came out with his deer rifle. "Just so you know," he taunted me, "you won't live to get out the door and neither will she."

So once again, I was eight months pregnant and all alone with a man who seemed to want us dead. I tried to reason with myself and again decided that Keith was an alcoholic and mentally ill and was self-medicating with alcohol. But that gave me no peace.

Chapter 3

When he was at home he was often angry and out of control, drinking to excess, cursing, ranting and raving for hours into the night. But for a time, he left the guns alone.

The Lord blessed us with a little boy. Keith was out driving a truck, so he missed this birth but did show up at the hospital hours later. Oddly enough, he was a proud father and took advantage of every opportunity to show off his children.

It wasn't long after our son's birth that his life spiraled down again. As usual his drinking escalated, and nothing could please him. He decided that he wanted to move. He quit his teaching job in the middle of the year, and we moved several hundred miles away to a small community where Keith's aunt and uncle lived. He had a close relationship with his cousins and always wanted to move to that area.

We bought ten acres of land from his uncle and put a mobile home on it. His cousin and her husband lived next door to us, and we became good friends. Her husband worked at the oil refinery and helped Keith get a job there. Keith had grown up around refineries because his dad worked in one most of his life so it seemed like a natural place for him to work. He tried to be content with what he did. The money was good, but I knew it bothered him because he felt like he was doing manual labor and that he had gone backwards in his career. For a brief time, our lives were quiet. Keith still drank every night to excess, but he left me and the children alone.

Unexpectedly, our lives changed again. Keith, who had always seemed to be able to keep his problems behind closed doors, suddenly found that his secrets were moving outside of our family. He was having trouble with friends and neighbors.

He and his cousin's husband drove back and forth to work together every day. One afternoon they were late getting home. They had gotten

Chapter 3

into an argument driving home and ended up pulling over and physically fighting it out. Our relationship with his cousin was never the same. That same month, he also had a big fight with his aunt and uncle over the land they sold us. The next week he physically attacked a neighbor over the use of the community well.

It seemed that it was becoming more difficult for him to keep up the pretense that he had so carefully nurtured for years. His insane behavior was reaching beyond our four walls. I was hopeful that others might become aware of Keith's problems, and that someone, somewhere would reach out to help us. But instead, his battles cost us the relationships around us that we so desperately needed and still did not bring any relief or help to myself or my children.

Chapter 4

ഔരു
"Thou art my hiding place; thou shalt preserve me from trouble; thou shalt compass me about with songs of deliverance. Selah."
Psalms 32:7

The insane nights became longer and less predictable. Keith seemed to be enough in control to keep his behavior together until the children were all in bed. Then he would get his pistol and threaten suicide. He would go back and forth trying to decide whether to kill me or kill himself. His behavior had taken on a new face of danger for all of us, and I felt a great fear

Chapter 4

of the one who was supposed to be protecting and caring for us.

The first time Keith held a gun to my head, I was terrified. I did not expect to live through the night. The next few times I was very frightened and still did not know if I would live through those nights. Finally, after so many times of feeling the gun barrel against my temple or my forehead or below my ear, I would still be afraid and that "what if" thought would pass through my mind. But eventually, the situation became a waiting game. I would wait until he passed out, and then I would get on with my life. Years later when I learned the truth, I had a very different emotion about those times. I realized that he really had wanted to kill me but God always kept him from pulling the trigger. I had witnessed life-saving miracles time after time.

I spent a lot of time in prayer, complaining and asking God to free us from this situation. I often prayed that Keith would die or that he would go ahead and end his life so that we could be free. And then I would feel such shame and horror that the thought would even cross my mind. No matter how fervent and agonizing my prayers were, God did not open doors for us to leave. In fact, He continually closed them.

I tried to talk to my family and friends about my fears, but nobody seemed to realize the danger we were in. Keith was so good at hiding his problem that everybody thought I was just sensitive to his drinking because of my Southern Baptist background.

I finally had enough and decided that I had to take the kids and get away. Keith and I had saved several thousand dollars, and I took $2000 and transferred that amount to a savings account in my name only. I planned to apply to a college and live on student loans until I could get a job.

Unfortunately, Keith discovered the change in our account before I had a chance to leave.

Chapter 4

He waited until the kids were in bed to discuss it with me. He had been drinking since he got home from work, and this time I at least understood his rage. He spent hours holding the gun to my head and threatening me. He would cry and curse me. That was when he promised me that if I ever took the children and left him, he would "hunt" us down and kill us all and then he would kill himself. He told me that he would see me dead if he ever thought I might leave him for someone else.

From that moment on, my feelings for him changed. Even though I had survived many difficult and life-threatening situations before this incident, I still felt a love for Keith. But now my love for him was turning to pity, and I was saddened at the person he had become. I know that I still loved a part of him, but I lost my passion for our life together. My quest became, not to keep our marriage and family strong, but to keep my children safe. I kept a hundred dollar bill, a credit card, and car keys in my pocket all the time. It didn't matter if I was doing laundry, cleaning the toilet, or working in the yard, I was always ready to make a quick escape. I knew that I was on my own and that I had to protect my children in any way I could.

Keith had applied at the high school and after struggling for eight months at the refinery, he was offered a job teaching business classes. He was overjoyed. He was back in a career that he loved and living in a place where he had always dreamed of living. We became active in a local church and again greatly enjoyed the fellowship of Christian friends. Keith took on the position of Sunday school director and eventually was nominated as a deacon in the church. He once again cut back on his drinking and even had those moments when he vowed to stop drinking altogether. He went as far as giving his testimony before the church, although it was filled with half-truths. I was also a leader in the wom-

Chapter 4

en's ministry and had such hopes that our lives were going to change. God was faithful in protecting the children and me, and we had several months of peace.

Keith decided that he wanted to get back into flying and still had his A & P license, so he opened an airplane mechanic business at the airport. I was working as a bookkeeper, and our finances were in good shape. One day he came home and told me that he was going to take on another part-time job, teaching college during the evening. He was working all day, three evenings a week, and all weekend. At least, I believed he was working. Now I can only imagine what he was doing during all of those hours.

Keith and I had been married eight years when the Lord blessed us again. It was quite a surprise when I discovered that I was pregnant again. God gave us another son. He was such a gift for me but I worried more about what his life would be like as he came into this dysfunctional family. I struggled to protect our three children and worried so much about all of them and what they had to witness and endure.

I continued to work as a bookkeeper and had to leave the children at daycare. When our baby was six weeks old, he took pneumonia and ended up in the hospital for several days. I decided to quit my job and stay home to care for the kids. After a month, I was offered a job at a preschool that allowed me to take all three of our children with me so we didn't have the added expense of daycare. I tried to never leave the children alone with Keith now. His behavior was too unpredictable, and I feared what he might do.

It was shortly after this that Keith decided he would build us a house. He had never been involved in construction work before, but he took on the job of building this house on his own. He did most of the work himself, although a few friends did help. Keith studied and tested for many of the required licenses. He was working full time at the high school, teaching and supervising a work–study program. He was teaching a college class two nights a week and was running his own airplane mechanic business at the airport, yet he still completed this house in three months.

When our son was eighteen months old, he had a grand-mal seizure and was eventually diagnosed with a brain tumor. This was a very difficult time for us. We took him for a second opinion and after traveling to a renowned children's hospital and running several more tests, we were told that they could not find a tumor but there was something unusual in his brain activity. He was prescribed medication, but after a year free of seizures, our family doctor took him off of all medications. He did not have any more problems.

During this time, Keith missed a lot of work and did a lot of drinking. I know he was worried about our son, but it was becoming more and more obvious that he was no longer able to deal with conflict. Maybe his guilt overwhelmed him, and he feared that God would take our son to punish him. The only thing I am sure of is that once more he found his escape from life in his alcohol.

Keith was sleeping only three to four hours a night. Somehow he was still able to make it to work and kept long hours there. When he was home, our lives were unbearable. His behavior was erratic, and he would sit with his pistol on his lap and threaten suicide or hold the gun to my head and threaten murder. He became so depressed at times but refused to go to the doctor or to confide in friends for help and support. I tried many times to convince him that he did not have to work his extra jobs but he was obsessed with staying busy.

For several months he struggled this way, but suddenly it all changed again. He didn't

Chapter 4

become the loving husband and father I kept praying for, but he began to sleep at night and his depression lifted. He continued to drink, but once again we were given a reprieve and there was more peace in our house.

Our next big crisis came one year later. One of the planes that Keith regularly performed maintenance on went down. There was an investigation, and the result attributed pilot error as the cause of the accident. But during the investigation, Keith was under such stress that he became very suicidal. He missed several days of work and spent those days drinking and in an alcoholic stupor. Again it was obvious that he was no longer capable of dealing with conflict.

During this time the kids and I would leave the house before he got up in order to be away from him. We would visit friends, go to the park, or just run around downtown. I did all I could to keep the children away from him as long as possible, and when we finally returned to the house, I prayed that he would be gone.

One evening we stayed at a friend's house for supper, and when we finally got home Keith was passed out in the living room. I got the kids bathed and in bed and got myself ready for bed, hoping that he would stay passed out for the rest of the night. But it was not to be. I had just crawled into bed and turned out the lights when he came stumbling down the hall and jerked me out of bed. He half-carried, half-dragged me down the hall and threw me on the sofa. He grabbed his .357, and once again I had it jammed against my forehead. I was more afraid this time. He had been drinking continually for four days and nights, eating and sleeping very little, and his behavior had been insane. I knew he was both mentally and physically out of control.

But I was also tired of all of this, and I grabbed a lamp and slammed it against his arm. The

Chapter 4

pistol slipped from his hand, and I was able to push it under the sofa before he could regain his balance. He came at me and pushed me hard against the fireplace. As I got back up his hands circled my throat, and he began to strangle me. Suddenly, all three children were in the living room screaming at him and jumping on his back, hitting him as hard as they could. While he was distracted I managed to free myself from him and hurried the kids out the door and into the car.

We spent the night at a friend's house. I did call the police, and they told me they would drive over and check it out. I don't know what he told them, but he was able to convince them that nothing had happened and he had just been having a hard time worrying about what might happen to his business. He convinced them that I was over-reacting and that nothing had actually happened. They did not contact me.

And so it continued for two more days. His nights were spent threatening suicide and threatening to kill me. I would will myself to just be quiet and wait it out. The kids were always in bed, and I prayed that they would stay asleep and not come out of their rooms. As the investigation into the accident ended and Keith realized that the cause of the accident was pilot error, he resumed his life as if nothing had happened.

Chapter 5

ೞಛ
*"Know ye not that they which run in a
race run all, but one receives the prize?
So run, that ye may obtain."
I Corinthians 9:24*

After the airplane incident Keith lost the small amount of control he had at home, and any conflict was met with rage and alcohol. There was no meaningful conversation. There was no husband–wife or father–child interaction.

He had been physically abusive before. He was physically abusive when he threatened me with the gun, and he did push me at other times. He had never struck me, but now he had attempted to strangle me. I hated that my children had to know, and I was horrified that they had tried to fight him off. But in all reality, I do not know what would have happened if they had not intervened. His violence had moved to a whole new level. And now my children had become actively involved in this battle.

I was so desperate. I knew that this was not God's plan for my life and especially not for my children's lives. I had to take some action. I did not know what to do next. I was sure that if the children and I left, Keith would search for us and we had no protection. There was no place we could go where we would be safe. He would find us, and I could not bear to think of what he might do to the children. I could not count on either set of our parents. I had tried that route many times and been turned down. I had involved the police and had no protection there.

I knew I had to do something, and then I remembered who was really in charge of our

Chapter 5

lives. I grabbed my Bible and fell to my knees. "Jesus, I am sorry that I have spent hours trying to solve this problem alone. I am sorry that I did not think to come to you first. I know you have always been right next to us during the worst of times and that you have promised not to leave us or forsake us. I don't understand the why of all of this but I know that you do. Guide me to do what I need to do. Protect us, Father. I give it all to you." After I prayed, I felt that peace that comes only from God. I still didn't know what I would do, but I knew that God would lead me. I was reminded that he was still in control of our lives, and that Satan had no power over us.

We were sitting in church the following Sunday morning, and our pastor's focus was on Acts 10:36-38. My heart focused on verse 38 and the words of Paul: "how God anointed Jesus of Nazareth with the Holy Spirit and with power, who went about doing good and healing all who were oppressed by the devil, for God was with Him." Our pastor was telling us how Jesus would forgive even the most horrid sins and redeem hearts that were repentant.

I felt that God was speaking directly to my family, reminding us that there was hope for Keith. He led me to speak to our pastor. I made an appointment with him for the following Wednesday. I did struggle greatly with this decision as Keith was still actively involved in church leadership and had been able to keep up his façade. I knew that I was exposing my husband's weaknesses and vulnerability.

On that Wednesday morning, I drove to the church with a burdened heart, but I knew that I was doing the right thing and that God had led me to our pastor. I spent an hour with him and told him about Keith's drinking and his suicide attempts. I told him that he had attempted to murder me and that things were becoming unbearable in our lives.

Chapter 5

He asked a couple of questions but mostly just listened to what I had to say. That afternoon he called my husband and told him that he would not be allowed to serve in the church as a deacon or as a Sunday school director because of his drinking problem. Unfortunately, that was the only help that came from our pastor. I spent several long nights dealing with Keith's threats and anger because I betrayed him and asked for help.

That was the end of my husband's church attendance in that community. Although, he no longer attended church, he was insistent that our children be in church every Sunday. Thankfully, God had instilled in my heart that my faith was not in the church but in Jesus Christ. Although I felt betrayed by my pastor, I knew that God had not forsaken me. That does not mean that I did not question God at times and sometimes even wondered why he led me to the pastor if there was no help there. I would have thoughts that He had deserted us. I would be angry with Him. But deep in my heart, I knew that He was always near. Too many times he had intervened in such obvious ways, and I knew He would not leave us alone.

Keith finished the house. It was a beautiful place, and we had lots of room. We were all very proud of our new home. We moved in, but it didn't solve any of our problems. We still lived in that surreal world of "off-and-on" insanity. Keith's behavior was becoming more bizarre, and he was having a harder time hiding "his secret."

When Keith was growing up, his family traveled a lot. They made yearly trips to Disneyland and often visited out-of-town family. My family, on the other hand, hardly ever took any trips. We were not close to any of our relatives but would see our grandparents once a year. But those visits were more of a chore than a vacation.

We seldom saw much of my family—partly because my father did not like to travel and

Chapter 5

partly because Keith did not get along with them. I talked Keith into traveling to visit my parents on a weekend. We planned to leave on a Friday afternoon. When Keith came in from work, I had loaded our luggage and had everything ready so we could leave immediately. But as he came in the front door, he was staggering, and I could tell he had been drinking. He must have left work early and had stopped at the bar. That was unusual because, as far as I knew, he did not spend time in bars but I knew he wouldn't be drinking at work.

I told him that we wouldn't go because he was in no condition to drive. The sparks flew as he reached over and put his hand on our daughter's shoulder and pulled her over to him. He looked at the kids and told them to go get in the car. But I was determined that this was one battle I would win. I walked out the door behind the kids and he followed me, slamming and locking the door behind him. I let him get into the vehicle and held the kids back beside me. Having my keys along with my $100 bill and credit card in my pocket, I turned around and took the kids back into the house. I explained to them that we were not going to go with him because it just wasn't safe. When he realized what was going on, he peeled out of the driveway. I breathed a prayer of thanks to God as I locked the front door. Not that I could keep him out but it was a positive action for me.

I didn't see him until four hours later. On Saturday morning he got up and said that he really wanted to go and that he wouldn't drink. My parents were expecting us so we headed out. As soon as we got fifty miles down the road he pulled his .357 out from under his seat. He drove the rest of the way with the .357 on his lap. Periodically, he pulled over and threatened to shoot himself, but this time he didn't threaten to shoot me. As we finally pulled up in front of my parent's house, I opened the car door and

Chapter 5

told the kids to go knock on the front door. Keith just sat there. As soon as they were safely at the door, I leaned over the seat as though to pick up my purse and grabbed the gun. I slammed the car door and hurried into the house. My father was standing near the front door and I handed him the pistol and asked him to hide it so Keith would not be able to find it. He did not ask me any questions but took the gun from me and put it up. I had hoped that he would realize that something major was wrong, but he never asked me about it. Two days later, when we were ready to go home, my father took the pistol and handed it back to Keith. Even though I was not surprised, I still felt betrayed by my father. He should have helped us. It was frustrating, but we did drive home without incident.

A couple of months later Keith was scheduled to sponsor a high school band trip to Disneyland. He left two days early, saying he had to get to California to complete some of the arrangements for the trip. I didn't question him as I was glad that we would have a few days of peace without him. Unfortunately, the very next day he called me from Las Vegas, asking me to fly out and meet him. He had been arrested and was in jail for a DUI. I, true to my enabling self, made arrangements for the kids to stay with their aunt and uncle and caught a flight out. Keith had gotten out of jail and met me at the airport. He was still very distraught over the situation. I knew that I had become his enabler and did not know how I could get myself out of that role.

"Why had I come?" I asked myself sadly. But I knew that I didn't want Keith to lose his job because I didn't know what would become of us. He would be home and insane all the time, taking things out on us. I stayed for one night and then flew back home. There were no repercussions for Keith except for a big fine.

Chapter 5

I was physically, mentally, and emotionally exhausted when I got home. I was so tired of struggling to make sense of what our world had become. I felt so helpless and so alone, and it seemed that there was no one who could help us. I cried out to God, "How can I go on this way? Please intervene. Please change our lives. I need your peace tonight." I knew I had to spend some in-depth time with God. Keith was still in California, so I knew we would have a peaceful night.

I got the kids into bed and grabbed my Bible and climbed the stairs. As I moved into the room, I began to pray. I paced back and forth across the room asking God for answers and begging Him to rescue us from this insanity. I could visualize bars surrounding me almost as though I were a tiger in a cage. For hours I paced and prayed. I ranted and I raved. I told Him it wasn't fair and that He had given me more than I could handle, even though He promised me that he wouldn't. I begged God to open doors and let me leave with the kids. Finally, I was spent. I simply fell to my knees and cried, sobbing so loudly I was afraid I would wake the kids. I finally pulled myself together and added a few more words to my prayers. "Forgive me for my lack of faith. I don't know what You see or what You are allowing, but I do know that You are with us and that You are in control of our past, our present, and our future. Give me peace and wisdom. Increase my faith."

I sat down and opened my Bible. God led me to Hebrews 12 and as I read, I knew He was telling me that I was not alone, that I was surrounded by a great cloud of witnesses. Then I read on and realized that I still had a race to finish. I knew He was telling me that it wasn't over yet.

Toward early morning, He answered my prayers with such a great peace penetrating my heart. I knew He would eventually free us,

Chapter 5

and I felt like He was telling me that everything would be okay. But I also heard Him as he was telling me that it wouldn't happen now. As I looked around the room, I could still clearly see the bars of the cage. With His still, small voice, He was telling me what I didn't want to hear. He was telling me to wait.

Chapter 6

ಸಂಖ
"Let no man say when he is tempted,
I am tempted of God: for God cannot
be tempted with evil, neither tempts he
any man: 14 But every man is tempted,
when he is drawn away of his own lust,
and enticed. 15 Then when lust hath
conceived, it brings forth sin: and sin,
when it is finished, brings forth death."
James 1:13-15

I was still working at the daycare center and was in charge of the preschool program. I was running late one day and ended up leaving some books at home that I needed at school. Classes were not being held at the public schools that day, and Keith was home. I called

Chapter 6

the house and asked him to bring the books to me and he told me that he would bring them by and just put them in my car.

An hour later I went out to the car to see if the books were there. There was a cloth draped over the steering wheel. It was wet and seemed to be covered with blood. The books I had asked Keith to bring to me were lying on the front seat. My first thought was that he had attempted suicide again, that he had slit his wrist. I raced back into the school and asked my assistant to take over the class for a while. I hurried home, dreading what I might find. Keith was not home, and I had no way of knowing where he was. I looked around and found no body and no blood so I decided that there was nothing I could do. I headed back to class and worked for the rest of the day.

After work, the children and I went home. Keith was there and I asked him about the bloody cloth but he denied knowing anything about it. I was never positive where the blood came from, but that same evening when we got home, our beloved collie was missing. We never found her.

A few weeks later I came home from work early in the afternoon and found that Keith was already home from school. I knew he had been home for hours as it was obvious that he had been drinking and was in a stupor. He had an almost-empty bottle of scotch sitting on the table beside him and an open beer in his hand. His pistol was sitting on the end table. As soon as I walked in he went into a rage, screaming, ranting, and raving. And then suddenly he was in tears, crying, and sobbing, moaning and groaning. The feeling of evil in the air was smothering. I stepped back away from him, grabbed the children and left the house.

Chapter 6

I took the kids to a friend's house. Her husband was a state policeman, and I told her the situation. I called Wayne, a close relative, and asked him to come over and help me. I went back to the house to wait for him. Wayne came in, and I could tell he was shocked at Keith's condition. This was the first time that I had asked for help and, even though he knew Keith drank too much, I don't believe that he knew about our problems.

I knew that Wayne avoided conflict. He had never learned how to deal with the trials that came into his life or the lives of those around him. I did not totally understand this at that time, but over the years I have come to better understand this about him. I do not regret calling him for help because, years down the road, he would be the one who would finally have the answers to my many questions.

Wayne told me to leave, and I went back to my friend's house. I called the house a couple of hours later to see if Keith had calmed down or passed out. While Wayne was on the phone with me, Keith went back to the bedroom and locked the door. When we finished talking, Wayne went back to the bedroom and knocked on the door. Keith would not respond. He finally had to kick the door open, and Keith was lying on the bed with the pistol in his mouth. Wayne could see him struggle and he knew that Keith wanted to die. He was in agony. Keith suddenly pulled the barrel from his mouth, unable to pull the trigger. Was he afraid to face God? At that moment Wayne moved over and took the pistol.

Suddenly Keith turned towards Wayne. Horrible words of confession poured vehemently from his mouth. Wayne was stunned. His head spun. He could feel his anger growing at this confession. But then just as suddenly he decided that Keith was trying to send him into a rage—a rage so insane that he would shoot Keith himself—suicide by someone else. Slowly

Chapter 6

he felt his blood pressure lowering, but he knew he could not stay with Keith any longer.

Wayne was a very private person and seldom shared his emotions or thoughts with anyone. This is how he was raised. He refused to believe this confession, and it would be many years before he spoke of it again. Since I learned the truth, I often wished he would have shared it with me that night. He would have spared the children and I so much more pain.

As this saga continued, we were still at my friend's home when her husband called. She told him what was going on, and he decided to go to our house. He walked around the back and listened to see if he could hear what was happening. He could hear Keith's ranting and raving and threats. He made the decision to call for back-up. Wayne saw him through the window and, still reeling from Keith's words, he stepped outside to let the state policeman know what was happening inside and told him that he was leaving.

Before the night was over, Keith had gotten the pistol back and fired it through the ceiling. Our house was surrounded by state policemen when he finally passed out. No one confronted Keith. They sat outside the house just waiting. After several hours most of the state police left also. Two officers stayed outside until early morning.

Early the next morning they called me and asked me to come over and see if Keith was still sleeping. They told me to bring the guns out if I could. I went in and he was still asleep, but woke up when I was getting the guns. He asked me what I was doing and I told him. He rolled over and went back to sleep. I was able to take the pistol and the rifles out to the officers. The next week Keith was able to pick them up and bring them home.

Chapter 6

I could not figure out what was behind all of this insane behavior. I knew whatever it was, it was serious. There was no talking to Keith about it. He exploded whenever I brought anything up. All he would say is that he was drinking and got out of control. There was no communication. Surprisingly enough for me, there were still no charges filed. It was as though nothing had happened at all, and life went on.

Today, I know why Keith was groaning and moaning and wailing. He had stepped across the line but this time with a close relative. I believe that up to this time he had been able to keep his secret life separate from family. I am convinced that this fear is what led to many of his conflicts with me. It is strange to realize that underneath it all Keith had a great fear of losing his family. But now, he had another fear. Someone close to us knew his secret, and this secret could cost him his freedom. He could end up in prison. All the individual had to do was talk.

He was haunted day and night for the rest of his life over this possibility.

Apparently the incident had happened the night before. I do not know if he was guilt-ridden for his sin or if he was just afraid that his secrets were now going to be discovered. His solution was to end his life. That seemed to be the solution that he always came back to but he just could never bring himself to follow through and pull the trigger. The cause of this violent episode would lay hidden to me for the next thirty years but would eventually be the key that answered so many of my questions.

Several months after that incident, my younger brother and his family, who lived out of state, planned to visit for the week. The day before, Keith got up at 5:00 a.m. and started drinking. By lunchtime he was very drunk. We had a long, hard day and night with guns and insanity and more drinking. We were up until 4:00 in the morning when he finally passed out.

Chapter 6

It was a Saturday but he got up at 7:00, dressed, got in his car and left without a word. He was not home when my brother and his family arrived, and I had no idea where he had gone. As usual, I made up several excuses and started supper. Our close relative, who now knew Keith's secret, came over. I invited her to stay for supper with us. She joined us in the kitchen and decided to make an apple pie. We were laughing and kidding around and having a great time together. She put her pie in the oven and when it was ready, I pulled it out of the oven and sat it on top of a burner that I thought was off. Unfortunately, it had been left on and as the pie plate heated up on this burner, it suddenly exploded. The shattered glass fell on to the kitchen linoleum and burned the floor covering. My brother's wife knew I was worried about it and was comforting me by telling me that, in the years to come, it would be a memory for me. I would always remember this day when I saw the burned floor!

Later, I wished the burned spot would be the only thing I remembered about that day.

When Keith finally came home he was staggering drunk. He came blundering into the house, cursing and yelling. I did not acknowledge him and tried to ignore his outbursts. He was out of control before anyone could speak to him. His behavior was unusual because he was always able to control himself when anyone else was around. When he walked into the kitchen and saw that "she" was there he became even more volatile. He was screaming that he was going to leave and went into the bedroom to pack his clothes. He walked towards the door still cursing me.

My brother, who had stood quietly by, finally had enough. He started towards him as Keith cursed me. But I reached out and stopped him and told him that we just needed to let him get out the door and away. He stood back because I had asked him to just let it go. But Keith continued to spew out profanity towards me until my brother finally heard all he could stand and told Keith to shut his mouth. Keith threatened him, and they both went outside to the front yard. A big fight ensued with the sheriff finally being called by the neighbors.

I was devastated and can remember the expressions on our neighbor's faces and the fear on the faces of our children as they watched. I can also recall the feeling of relief that I no longer had to keep our problem hidden. It was out in the open. But in spite of my hopes, no help came and nothing in our situation changed.

That Christmas I invited Wayne and his family to come for Christmas dinner. Keith agreed reluctantly. But when the holiday arrived, Keith got up early, dressed, and told me that he had a high school tournament that he had to attend. He left the house and was gone until late that evening. We all knew that there would be no tournament held on Christmas Day. I was thankful for his absence, but it was still embarrassing to explain. I had to make excuses because I didn't know what was going on, but Wayne knew. Keith had already confessed a very serious part of his secret to Wayne. Even if Wayne had chosen not to believe the confession, it still had to come up to the surface when he was around Keith. How could Keith sit face-to-face with this man in light of what Wayne knew?

Sadly enough, these incidents didn't seem to affect Keith. His addiction and his secret had taken over, not only his life, but our lives as well. I lived with a sad, pathetic shell of a man whose whole life now focused on "his secret."

We seldom shared the holidays with our parents since our early years of marriage. But after this incident we became even more isolated from any family and friends. Whenever family came to our house for holidays or just for visits, Keith would disappear. This happened without fail. Sometimes he would tell me he

Chapter 6

had to work, and other times he would just get up early and leave and I had no idea where he was. His behavior before and after these visits was always bizarre and out of control. So it was up to me to face family and friends and make excuses for his disappearance. He was hiding in fear because someone besides Wayne knew his secret, and he always had the fear that one day it would all come out. He had no idea how many others had been told.

As the years have passed, I have often reflected as to why I stayed with Keith and have struggled with that question. Much of my pain has come from the fact that I exposed our three children to this torment. I felt that I had made the choice, but they were the innocent victims. During the first year, I knew I loved Keith and I could not imagine a life without him. After our third year of marriage, I struggled to feel any love for him. He had become so violent, and I believed he was capable of anything. I truly believed that if we left him, he would find us and kill us all. I knew those things happened. And I knew that if I were to leave him, I would have to be hiding my children and on guard all the time and ready to defend all of us to the point of death—his or mine.

He had built up such a strong reputation in the community, and people loved and admired him so greatly. Even if there had ever been the possibility of divorce, I knew he would have a chance of partial custody of the children. I could never put them in a place where they would be alone with him. Ironically, I knew I could protect the children much better if I was there with him.

Chapter 7

"They that trust in the LORD *shall be* as mount Zion, *which* cannot be removed, *but* abides forever."
Psalm 125:1

Keith completed his master's degree and received his administrative certification. He applied for an assistant principal job at a high school in a small community located about twenty miles from where we lived. It was his dream job and just exactly the position that he had been working towards for years. This job was a big promotion for him and one that he really wanted.

We planned to travel up the coast during summer vacation. Our vacations gave us a break from our everyday lives, and Keith was always insistent that we take a vacation every summer. The first couple of years, our vacations were real getaways. Keith would not get drunk, and we would have a wonderful time. Even later he would be able to relax more when we traveled and, although he would drink, he seemed to control his behavior so much more than when he was home. Sometimes our vacations would be the only happy time in our lives.

What made me think that we could survive two weeks on the road without an incident, escapes me. Maybe it was the fear that he would force the children into the vehicle, and I would be helpless to stop him. I had lost faith in calling for help and legally he had a right to have the children with him.

We ended up in Oregon and decided to spend the day at one of the beaches. Up to this

Chapter 7

point, things had been okay. We put up a little tent for the kids and sat up some chairs. Keith sat down, a scotch in one hand and a book in the other, while the kids and I played in the water and built sandcastles. He was drinking heavily, and I knew things were going to get worse. I focused on staying close to the kids, touching my back pocket to insure that I had my credit card and hundred dollar bill tucked away.

It was in mid-afternoon when Keith began to complain about the noise the kids were making. The situation escalated from there. Finally, he jumped into the pickup and took off. I was a little confused because I had not expected him to leave but thought that the kids and I would have to deal with his anger.

Momentarily I was relieved but then I realized that we were now stranded on the beach. My first thought was that we could sleep in the tent but then I realized how insane that thought was. I had my credit card so I knew we would be able to get back home. I decided that I would not panic, but we would just keep enjoying our time at the beach until we had to ask for help getting into town. I almost hoped that he would not come back for us.

Fortunately, I had unloaded the ice chest from the pickup earlier so we sat down about 5:30 and had sandwiches for supper. About two hours later Keith pulled back in with no explanations. Without a word he loaded everything up, and we headed into town to find a campground. Where had he gone and what had he done? This question haunts me more now than it did at that time.

The next day he called his office and heard that he had been hired for the job as principal. His whole attitude changed. He went for two straight days only drinking two six-packs. But his euphoria didn't last long, and he started drinking heavily the next night. I did not have much hope with this new position. I knew that

Chapter 7

he had started a lot of new things before. His life would only change for a brief time if it changed at all. He had spent years traveling down the wrong path. There were many times I wondered if he had sold out to the devil? I could not see him changing.

He had reservations for the next day for deep-sea fishing and was drunk when he left us. We were parked at a campground nearby so the kids and I had the pickup. We had a great day without him as we were near a beach and a park area. Toward early afternoon, it became very stormy. He was late coming back, so the kids and I went into a restaurant nearby and enjoyed an early supper. We were so at peace that I found myself wishing that he would fall overboard and be lost at sea and not come back. I always felt tremendous guilt when I had these thoughts but I was beginning to have them often now.

He was at the pickup when we finally returned. He wasn't happy when he didn't find us waiting and did not know where we were. We struggled through another evening of insanity.

Finally, it was time to head for home and we drove straight through, stopping only briefly to eat. The kids slept in the back, and Keith and I took turns driving and sleeping. We survived another vacation and made it back home.

Chapter 8

ಲಂಡ
"Fear thou not; for I *am* with thee: be not dismayed; for I *am* thy God: I will strengthen thee; yea, I will help thee; yea, I will uphold thee with the right hand of my righteousness."
Isaiah 41:10

Keith started his new job, and for a short while our lives were fairly calm. He developed a great rapport with his teachers and staff and students. He had a lot of charisma and was usually very popular with his coworkers. He worked hard and somehow was still able to hide his other self when he was on the job.

Although we only lived about twenty miles from where his new school was, he insisted that we move. He decided to build another house. He hired a contractor this time and had several men helping with the work. He cut back on his drinking, and I could tell it was a struggle for him. He fought constantly with the contractor and the builders and continued to take his anger and frustration out on me. We bought a small camper and moved it to the new house, so that he could be there more. Our living quarters were tight, but he was out working most of the time so the kids and I often had times of peace. God moved quickly and we sold our other home, so we did not have the stress of two mortgages.

He was doing well in his job and really enjoyed the work, but I could tell he was still battling his demons. He had no peace in his life and so the children and I had no peace in our lives either.

Chapter 8

The house was finished, and we were settled in by Christmas time. It was a strange time because Keith was not drinking as much but his behavior was very strange. He still had a lot of rage. He would often sit in the den moaning and groaning. There were times that he would wail as though he were in great pain.

We seldom entertained because our lives were so chaotic. But that Christmas Keith wanted to invite several of his colleagues over for a Christmas get together. The evening started out enjoyable, but before long several of the men were drunk, including Keith, and it wasn't long before bedlam reigned. One of the men sat down in one of the dining room chairs and somehow managed to fall over into the wall. He knocked a large hole through the wall. That was our last party.

My parents and my younger sister and her baby girl came up to visit after New Year's Day. My parents stayed with my brother and his family, and my sister stayed with us. Keith drank the evening away and became very violent and once again out of control. My sister was terrified. We loaded the children up and drove to a motel for the night. I called my brother from a pay phone and told him what was happening and that we were going to have to spend the night away from the house. Keith called my brother's house several times during the night, threatening him because he would not tell him where we were. My brother finally took his phone off the hook. We were left alone to fend for ourselves. My family left the following day.

Keith's job was high pressure, and it didn't take long for things to build up again. The high school principal decided to retire at the end of the year. Keith was being considered as his replacement but someone else with more experience was hired for the job. He was devastated and his insane behavior and drinking magnified.

Chapter 8

One Saturday, Keith got up saying he had to work. It was unusual because he did not work on weekends unless there was some activity or athletic event at the school. There was neither. I had already made commitments for the children to attend a birthday party, so I drove him to work as his pickup was in the shop.

It was late during the day when he called me for a ride. I drove to the school, and he was standing outside in the parking lot. As I drove up to him, I rolled down my window, and he began to scream and yell at me. He was in such a rage that his words made no sense. He had a coffee cup in his hand, and he suddenly threw it against the side of the car. I was really frightened, and the kids began to cry. We drove away without waiting for him. He arrived home about thirty minutes later, out of breath. He had run all the way home. He did not say a word about the incident—not then or ever. He got a drink, sat down, and drank himself into oblivion. His façade was crumbling.

He now spent his life after work, sitting in his recliner drinking. He would get up and eat supper and then head right back to his chair and his drinks. It was after the kids were in bed that he would lose control. With slurred obscenities, many of which I couldn't understand, he would rant and rave for hours. Then the guns would come out, and he would begin the threats of suicide and murder.

One of the most frightening fixations that began to occur was the laments that emanated from deep within his body. The moaning and wailing seemed to come from the depths of Hell and the ominous sound was terrifying sometimes becoming so loud that neighbors would call.

I don't know how any of us survived or why things didn't escalate further, but I soon learned that if I just kept quiet I would avoid a lot of

Chapter 8

physical violence. If I got up and tried to go to another room, he would follow me. I was always afraid that would put him closer to the children's' rooms so I would just sit quietly with him and pray. I used to pray that he would pass out or die from alcohol poisoning, but neither happened. He would finally go to bed, and I would lay there waiting for him to fall asleep. When he would finally sleep, I would take my pillow and sleep in the hall between the kids' bedrooms. I feared for my children and was afraid even to sleep any more.

The next day would come, and we wouldn't talk about it because there wasn't anything left to say—and his apologies and excuses just didn't seem to matter anymore. He was losing the strong control that he had always had and his weaknesses were beginning to grow.

Chapter 9

ಬಂಜ
"Now the Lord is that Spirit: and where the spirit of the Lord is, there is liberty."
I Corinthians 3:17

*E*ven when things seemed to be going well for Keith at work, he could not keep things together. He had his dream job and was well loved and honored, but his secret was eating away at him. I could tell that there was never any peace in his life now, not at work or at home.

He fell into a deep depression. He became unresponsive and missed a couple of days of

Chapter 9

work, spending both days drinking. I tried to convince him to let me take him in to see our doctor, but he shoved me out of the way and told me to leave him alone. The second evening I bathed the kids and got them in bed and then I got ready for bed.

I went into the den to see if Keith was still awake and found him sitting on the couch with the barrel of his deer rifle in his mouth. He was pressing against the trigger with a wooden ruler. I had hidden the .357 Magnum a few days before, hoping that he would not notice that it was gone. Apparently he didn't because he never looked for it or asked me about it. Even knowing that he had been severely depressed for the last few days, I was still not prepared for the nightmare that was ahead.

Thinking of this situation years later, I am sure that something occurred at his work place. He might have been caught in a compromising situation. I know that something happened because of this reaction. Looking back, I know that this was how he handled every situation caused by his secret. He was having a harder time living his double life. Possibly someone else discovered his secret, and it was time to run and hide again, or as he would think, to escape through suicide.

I tried to take the rifle from him but he slammed the rifle butt against my chest. He threatened to pull the trigger if I did not leave the rifle alone. Then he turned the rifle towards me and began to moan and sob so violently that I feared the kids would wake up and come running into the den and we would all die. I didn't know how I would be able to protect them from him. I cried out to the Lord to intervene and take care of us all. But I found no peace and could do nothing as I stared down the rifle barrel. He cursed me and suddenly broke down again. He cried uncontrollably all the time, keeping the rifle pointed at me. He told me to sit down while he

Chapter 9

figured out what he had to do. Suddenly he spun the rifle around and put it in his mouth again. He was moaning in agony. The moans came from deep inside of him and were loud and evil sounding. I felt helpless and feared that this was how our lives would end. Just as suddenly the sobs stopped and his eyes filled with hatred as he twisted the rifle around to point it back at me. I knew that I couldn't overtake him and that I had to wait until he wasn't focused on me. An hour passed, and his moans began to subside and quiet fell upon us.

It didn't last long as the shrill of the telephone broke through the horror of the moment. He picked up the phone, and his mother was on the line. It was late for her to be calling, but I felt such a relief thinking that she might sense the problem and talk him out of it. It was obvious that he was drunk, and he was still crying as he spoke to her. He kept the rifle pointed at me. From hearing his side of the conversation, I thought she was telling him that he needed to go to bed and sleep it off. He laughed at her and told her he was tired of living and that he was going to end it all right then. His voice changed, and it sounded like he was talking to his dad. He talked for almost an hour; sometimes he was coherent but mostly just mumbling and crying. I don't know what they were telling him, but he finally yelled at them telling them to stay out of his life. He hung up the phone.

He moved back to the couch where he still had a bottle of scotch sitting on the floor. He reached down and grabbed it and drank like he couldn't get enough. Once again I prayed that he would pass out, but he never lost his hold of the rifle. For another two hours he struggled with his decision, putting the rifle in his mouth and just as suddenly turning it on me. I sat quietly hoping and praying that I would find a chance to take the weapon.

Chapter 9

Finally, he tried to stand up, still holding the rifle, but he lowered it for just a moment. I twisted around and grabbed the barrel and jerked it out of his hand. At the same time I pushed him and he fell backwards onto the sofa. I ran to the back door with the rifle, planning to hide it in the wood pile. As I reached out to push the door open, I paused. "He wants to die and he has for a long time. I will just help him," I thought. I turned back around and held the rifle in front of me and walked back into the den. As I was aiming the rifle at him, I suddenly felt the pressure of a hand on my shoulder and heard a quiet voice reminding me that God was in control and He would handle this mess.

I came to my senses and realized what I was doing. It was then that I felt such a peace come over me, and my fear left me. I turned back and headed outside and threw the rifle into the wood pile. I hurried back in and found him on the floor moaning and crying in a voice that no longer sounded human.

The phone rang again and I rushed over to answer it. It was his mother calling back. I quickly explained the situation. She wanted me to meet them, and let them help me get him to a treatment center. I told her that I knew I would not be able to handle him to even get him in the car.

Suddenly, he got up from the floor and came over and took the phone from my hand. He spoke quietly with his mother and then gave me back the phone. "I'll go," he said. His mother told me that they would meet us halfway. I told her I thought I should call the police because he was in such bad shape and I didn't think I could handle him in the car. She begged me not to and told me that if I would just get him down to them they would get help for him.

By this time, it was after one in the morning. I quickly dressed and packed clothes for all of

Chapter 9

us. I woke up the children and got them into the car. After we were all loaded and ready I asked Keith to come and get in the car so we could head out. He just laughed and told me that he had decided not to go. He didn't care what I said or did.

I did the only thing I knew to do. I cried out again in prayer. "Please resolve this, Lord. There is nothing more I can do." Then I turned to him and told him that I would call and let his parents know. Suddenly he changed his mind and got into the front seat of the car. I started backing out of the garage. He threw the door open and said he could not go without something to drink on the way. He stumbled over to a shelf in the garage and grabbed a bottle of whiskey from one of his hiding places.

We had 180 miles to go to meet his parents, and I was not sure I could even get out of the garage with him in the car. All during the trip, he kept opening the door and threatening to jump out. I would reach over and grab him and hold him until I was able to pull the car over and get him back in with the door shut. My poor children just sat quietly the whole way. It took us four hours to go 180 miles but we finally met his parents. I felt nothing but relief to be able to turn him over to them. My plan was to drive back home with the kids, but when Keith realized my intention he refused to get into the car with his mom and dad. I finally agreed to follow them to the hospital which was another 160 miles away.

His parents struggled with him all the way just as I had. But we made it to the hospital at 9:00 that morning after a terrifying stop-and-go ride. Thankfully the kids slept most of the way, so they were spared some of their dad's behavior.

My plan for returning home went up in smoke. The doctors and nurses working with Keith convinced me that he would do better if I were involved in the program with him. My

Chapter 9

in-laws brought their camper and placed it in a site near the hospital. I didn't want to stay there without the kids, so we put them in the Christian school close to his parents. I thought this would be an easier transition for them since I only planned to be gone for a month, and I felt better that they would have the compassion of Christian teachers and leaders.

I called and spoke with Keith's boss and told them what was happening. His new boss suspected something was going on. The school board gave him leave and committed to holding his job for him. He was so well liked and respected for the job he did. He received over a hundred letters and cards from the staff, faculty, and students during his stay in the treatment center.

Once again I found a little hope. He had not gone through any rehabilitation programs and had never admitted to having a problem with alcohol. But now he was doing both, even though he had been forced into entering the treatment center. Maybe we would get to the bottom of his problem and he would find healing.

Chapter 10

ಐರ
*"For we wrestle not against flesh and blood,
but against principalities, against powers,
against the rulers of the darkness of this world,
against spiritual wickedness in high places."*
Ephesians 6:12

A lot happened during those weeks but nothing permanent was accomplished. The children and I did the best we could, and I tolerated being separated from them, hoping and praying that our lives would change.

I decided to share the time spent in the treatment center through our journals. I will let Keith tell his own story of that time through his journal, which was a requirement in his program. Parts of Keith's journal were corrected to make it more readable but I tried to leave most of it as it was written. My journal entries just gave me a chance to vent. It is easy to see that I was struggling to be supportive.

4/5/1984 Keith's journal

Entered/Special Care Day 1. Today was worthwhile.

4/5/1984 My journal

We had a nightmare trip. Keith kept opening the door trying to jump out of the car. He was so drunk and out of it. My poor kids. What a horrible life I have allowed him to make for all of us. I wish I could just leave him here and take the kids and go away. I want to let his mom

Chapter 10

and dad have him back. I know they don't want him, either. We arrived at the hospital at 9:00 this morning His mom and dad were with us.

Keith had his last drink at 4:00 this morning and was still disoriented and drunk. It angered him when the nurse took inventory of his personal belongings. He went crazy when she told me to take his money and his credit cards. He threw his wallet at me and told me to take it all. He complained about having a roommate. I had gone to the kitchen to get some coffee, and he came rushing into the room yelling and demanding that I get him his own room. He stayed angry all day. The nurses asked me to stay or I would have taken off. His mom and dad left with the kids and went back to their house. I pacified him. He kept saying that he did not have to put up with this regardless of what "you or Mother" say. Finally I left. He had a run-in with a nurse about getting his medication. They did medicate him as he was so out of control. He said he asked her several times for more meds, and she told him she would have to call the doctor. He said that she waited three or four hours before she finally brought him anything and told him she had other things to do. This was probably one of the best nurses because she wouldn't put up with his garbage. She said he kept trying to get dressed to leave. He called his mother three times after I left. I was just thankful that somebody else had to deal with him now. Maybe somebody will finally realize how dangerous he is, and we will be saved from this nightmare. I wish I knew that he would leave us alone. I would leave him

Chapter 10

in a second. I hate it that I am forced to be supportive right now. Even if he quits drinking I don't want to be around him.

4/6/1984 Keith's journal

Special care Day 2. Today was also worthwhile although not as beneficial as yesterday. Maybe things will work out here.

4/6/1984 My journal

I came back to the hospital. Keith was groggy and disoriented but seemed to be a little more in control today. He still wouldn't be quiet about being in prison. He was angry about everything, but at least he was not just yelling and cursing. He was still on medication. He was really nervous acting and kept saying he was bored. He said there was nothing to do and the four walls kept closing in on him and that he was tired of walking up and down the halls. He complained about everything and everybody. He just got more negative and angry as evening came. He was worried that he would not be able to sleep and that the nurses would not give him any medication to help. He was out of control and focused so much on not sleeping. He kept threatening to leave, so the nurse finally asked if I would stay a while longer. As soon as he heard I was going to stay, he calmed down. I talked to the nurse on night shift when she came in and told her I didn't think I should stay any longer. I told her that Keith calmed down when he was told I would stay, and I thought he was manipulating the situation. She called the counselor, and together they decided

Chapter 10

that it would be better if I left. Keith was already asleep so he didn't know I left.

4/7/1984 Keith's journal

Special Care Day 3

I screwed up. I did not need medication but thought it would help me sleep. I thought it all counted against my twenty-eight days. Found out that the twenty-eight-day count did not start until I went off special care. Was not told this until today and when I was told, I got off all medication.

4/7/1984 My journal

Today is Saturday. I wished I could just spend the day with the kids, and we could forget about Keith and his problems. But we loaded up and headed to the hospital. We got there at 8:15 after stopping at McDonald's for pancakes. We brought the food with us. I stopped and told Keith, we were there. He was in the bathroom. The kids and I went on into the kitchen to eat breakfast. At 8:30 his mom and dad came in. Keith was still in his room but came in right after they did. We watched a movie in the main room. Keith seemed to be really drugged and groggy. I asked the nurses about it, and then they became concerned and thought he had gone out to our car and found some alcohol there. But as far as I knew he hadn't been to the car and didn't have the keys but he did stay in his room a long time. I don't think there was any alcohol in the car but he always hid it everywhere so there might have been. One of the counselors went out and searched the car. If something

Chapter 10

had been there, Keith had gotten it. His mom and dad left early and took the kids with them. I wish they would have stayed, and I could have left with the kids. Keith thinks he can't stand this, but I don't know if I can stand much more of him either. I just want to get the kids and get away from him. He went to sleep and I left.

4/8/1984 Keith's journal

Special Care Day 4

All these days were worthless but didn't know it. The twenty-eight days won't start until the 9th when I will be released from all the medication.

4/8/1984 My journal

I drove home today to close up the house, get more clothes, and to get the dog. I was hoping that the kids and I could just go back home and stay, but the hospital program director said that I needed to be involved on a daily basis. The house was the same. I didn't see anybody around the neighborhood or any of my friends ... just packed up and closed up the house. I spent the night as I needed to be there on Monday to check the kids out of school. I got up early and got everything packed, checked the kids out of school, and had the mail forwarded. I couldn't believe how supportive the principals and secretaries at the kids' schools were. They sure do not know the kind of person he really is. He has so many people completely fooled. I finished and headed back. I wanted to get back to the kids. Keith's sister had them, so I didn't worry

Chapter 10

so much about them. They always like to be with her family.

4/9/1984 Keith's journal

My time for the twenty-eight days starts today.

EXERCISE:

Subject	Where do you stand? Now	Where would you like to be?	What steps to take?	When?
Drinking/ Using	*I do not drink.*	*Sober the rest of my life*	*Try to never take another drink*	*4/9/1984*
Family	*Close relation- ship but not close enough*	*As a bonded unity*	*Stop drinking, open up emotionally and let them know how much I love them*	*Now*
Employ- ment	*Adminis- trator for the Schools*	*Either an airline pilot or superin- tendent of schools*	*Job experience and education*	*Soon as I get out*

Finances	Upper Middle class, $35,000–40,000	Money really doesn't mean that much to me as long as I can support my family comfortably.	Pay raises, promotions, or change of occupation	When the current time and opportunity arises
Emotional	Stable with myself and my Lord	More emotionally stable with my peers and my wife	Understand that I can't do it all. I have to share my feelings more with both wife and peers	Starting Now
Spiritual	Very close relationship	Where I'm at unless the Lord has other plans	Continue to follow in His footsteps and provide better testimony to those who may be lost	Now

Chapter 10

Social Life Recreation	Right now not very good—Generally I have a very good social life within my community	Same social life but with different style, cold sober	Try my very best to never take another drink of alcohol	Now
Education	Master of Arts Degree/ working on PhD	Doctoral stage	Complete practicum and dissertation	Now
Other Personal	Realization of what is alcoholism	Sober for the rest of my life	Never take another drink	4/9/1984

4/9/1984 My journal

I went back to the treatment center after I visited with the kids and dropped the dog off. Keith was in the middle of a group session. I went into the kitchen as his older sister and husband were there visiting and waiting to see him. Keith came in all upset. He said the group was accusing him of sneaking out to the car and having something to drink. I think he did, so it was hard for me to listen to him. The nurses told me that they always come down hard on each other at first. I thought he needed them to do that. It would be just like him to find something to drink and to drink it with all the meds he was taking. He was so mad at me because he thought I should be defending him. Sadly, those days are over.

4/10/1984 Keith's journal

Day 2: Today was better. What one of the guys said about his problems seems to make mine small. I believe I can get something from this program. I believe I can get help here!! I had one decent session today, but I had already had most of this in my educational psych class in college. Last session was worthless. I didn't

Chapter 10

feel that the counselor should have come down on everybody as he did. As all educators know, no one gets 100% and all the instructor can do is offer his best— then it is up to the student to take the ball and run. We just read progress reports and then got a real unnecessary "ass chewing." As the sessions go, I enjoyed the recovery process and defense mechanism. Went to AA meeting at 8:00, and that, too, was senseless. All they said was how good AA was, but what do they do from Tuesday to Tuesday? I really miss my wife and the kids. From my observation of the last three days (and if the rest are like these), than actually no more than two weeks should be required to help the person stop drinking. We are many times repeating ourselves, which in my opinion is dumb! One can only learn how the other became a drunk so many times, and then it gets very boring. My anniversary is today. My wife is on her way, and I do desperately need her. My most meaningful thought is to be with my wife. I feel lonely. Right now I feel like just leaving. My anniversary night and I am incarcerated here with my wife and family so many miles away. I feel as if I can't stand it!! (I need to listen to some stress tapes now so must go.) 1:58 a.m. END

4/10/1984 My journal

It is our fourteenth anniversary today and not much worth celebrating. My marriage has not been the happily-ever-after life I had dreamed of. I do have the three kids to celebrate. I don't feel like I love Keith anymore. I just feel so sorry for him and I am accepting the responsibility to help

Chapter 10

him get better. I wish he would become well; then we could leave without the fear of him coming after us with the guns again. Keith gave me a nightgown that his mother bought. I didn't get him anything. It seemed kind of pointless. I am sure that hurt his feelings but my heart was not into celebrating an anniversary. I drove the group to the AA meeting that night and then I drove back to his mom and dad's. On the way I started worrying that he would just leave the program. When I got to the house, I told his mother that I was afraid he was not going to stay in the program. She told me that it did no good to worry about it. If he left the program, we would just do something else.

4/11/1984 Keith's journal

My wife came by tonight, but we didn't get out of session until almost 9:00 and we didn't have much time to visit. During the group meeting this afternoon we were able to share our emotions about the program. Now I'm not saying this program doesn't work. It just let me (us) get a little dissention out. I had a very disturbing day today. Mostly all we talked about was a sixth sense or the human spirit leaving the body and doing stupid miracles (those such as Satan). I tried to defend the Bible and my beliefs but know too little to quote scriptures and so on. The counselor believes he has the power to leave his body and predict or describe stuff such as articles of clothing that his girlfriend, who is miles away, was wearing when he has not seen or talked

Chapter 10

with her. I feel this morning and afternoon were wasted for me for I know of a spiritual being—a higher power—God. I did not need the theologies exercise that was given. There was a lot of Satanism discussed all day, and I don't care for this type of lecture. I am here to determine why or what is causing my drinking problem, not to listen to somebody tell me that what the Bible says has been misinterpreted. It was said we should read the book of Solomon (not the Bible book) and the "Book of the Dead" and that magic is religion. Religion to me is believing in God and trying to follow in His footsteps. Anyway, there was much more discussed about something called a "third eye" and its powers over the natural happenings of today's world. I see myself as a true full-fledged Christian of the Baptist denomination. So I just quit listening. I really couldn't convince them the Bible was written by God, that is, letters to and from Peter, Paul, John, and so forth, so I gave up. Oh, yes, this counselor stated that he got mad at his girlfriend one day, so he began transcendental thoughts (thinking real hard). And before he began his trance, it was a beautiful day. But the harder he thought and let his spirit out, the clouds formed. It rained very hard until she had to come in, and then the weather just cleared right back up. He swore to us this happened. Then he told us of another time he made the same thing happen again just to prove to her he could do it. This place is crazy. All I have done is tell everybody here I am an alcoholic, why, when I started drinking, and they in turn have told me the same. I've got the psychological help to determine if my problem is stress, location of

Chapter 10

residency, incompetence, or whatever. I could go to the preacher and tell him I'm alcoholic and get more results. I'm going to try to stick it out although it may drive me completely over the cliff, but if another day occurs such as today, I am leaving. I don't care who says what about it. By the way, the counselor has all his birds named after all the different gods of different cults (religions). 1:02 a.m. END

Not End: I know this sounds crazy and I can hardly believe it myself but it is really happening. I learned today how good a real Christian I am and how much I believe in the Bible. END (after reading what I wrote) 1:17 a.m. END

4/11/1984 My journal

Same old thing today. Keith was upset about his sessions with one of the counselors. He complained about "black magic." I couldn't help him much as I can never believe how much of what he says is true.

4/12/1984 Keith's journal

12:21 a.m. Well, another day has come and passed. (Thank God) It was not all that bad today because we did have some lecture although I have already had everything presented in college, that is, planning itineraries, problem solving, how to determine time wasters, and so on. But, what the hell, at least we weren't having to listen to how many times each of us got loaded or drunk or whatever.

Chapter 10

Yesterday I started thinking very seriously about why I began drinking and finally after hours of deliberation, it finally came to me, but I'll get into that in a moment. A very strange thing happened today after the first afternoon session, the counselor stated that he felt we needed a break from all the hard work we've been doing and asked if we would like to just enjoy and laugh for an hour or so. Of course, we all said yes so he left the room. Upon returning, he had a tape in his hand and proceeded to tell us about George Karlin. I've never listened to G. Karlin in my life and never plan to again. It was the most obscene, abusive tape I've ever heard. The man started off with something like, "There are 400,000 words in the human language—now only seven are not allowed on TV—(then he made some sort of dirty joke). And all of *a sudden he said "and they are ____, _____, and so forth. (I'll not go into detail.) From this he made what was supposed to be jokes about _____, _____, _____, and Lord knows what else. This is supposed to be a session on how to determine why I am an alcoholic. I do not see the relativity in this. This is supposed to be funny (not hardly). Anyway, besides the day's occurrences, I have made some very serious decisions. As of 4/9/1984, I will never (taken in context) take another drink. This is a solemn oath to God Himself. With His help, I can conquer anything. Also, I, myself, have come to the conclusion of the why I started drinking heavily. I feel I may not be in the best career for me. I have always loved flying and made a heavy decision many years ago that to have time with my family, education would be best. This* *probably was not the best decision for I have always missed flying. Anyway, I also saw that I was always doing things for any and everybody but did not realize the reason why. Now I can see why. It is because I need that feeling that they think I can do anything, and I need that feeling of importance in their eyes. It is now time to take off the mask and just be me. I don't have to do anything for anybody—just me. I set a goal a few years back to become an administrator in education. I have accomplished that goal. In fact, I am the youngest administrator in the state. I have met my goal, but I am not necessarily satisfied. And if I want to change, then I'm going to. Also, I need to show more of my true feelings (not necessarily emotions) but feeling toward my wife, my family, and all my loved ones. Now I know that this is just now in the decision process and I have a lot of hard work ahead of me to bring these things to light, but at least I have come to reality with myself and can start the implementation process. By the way, I met with a psychologist today, and her notes and thoughts correlated exactly with mine. She feels I have the mental ability, with some special books to study, to handle this situation on my own. I feel the same, although I want to meet with her at least one time and I feel my wife needs to, also. Maybe we need a joint meeting sometime prior to my departure from this hell hole. May I add this, there are mostly very good nurses here, and nurse aides, but there are also a couple that could use some constructive leadership techniques. The counselors (or so called counselors) are a total disruption to the program. There is one counselor in training who I feel will make a good counselor. One of the male counselors doesn't seem to be a bad counselor but I really don't know because I've never seen him do anything. I've got to go. It is after 2:00 a.m. and I need some rest for the exciting day tomorrow. 2:09 a.m. END*

4/12/1984 My journal

Keith seemed a little more rational today. Maybe after a week, he is finally deciding to work at this. We went to the AA meeting this afternoon. I thought it was good, but Keith felt it was all repetitious. It made me wonder if he is just playing games to manipulate again. He did not put much effort into the session but was eager to complain.

4/13/1984 Keith's journal

12:05 a.m.

Well, I don't have my date sheet to mark off the number of days, but I believe it is Day 5 or 6. My wife took it with her last night and failed to return it or a copy of it today. Today was totally uneventful with the exception of a film we saw on love and hate and how hate can destroy a person if it is carried within long enough. This morning we had a review of the week's learning given by a trainee. She reread the notes that had been read to us for the past week and then ended the session with a film before lunch. At 2:00 we had the psychologist come in and direct a session on our feelings of where we are, what we want, and when. We also gave one of the other clients his

Chapter 10

first step. By the way, this session was handled very professionally and very well as for us getting one of the other clients to open up and talk. This ended about 3:30 and that is all we did all day. I did go down and do some PT for about twenty minutes. Otherwise, I just waited around for time to pass. I want to stop wasting time. Visiting hours were at 5:00, and I was expecting my wife and kids but they did not arrive until sometime after 6:00. I was beginning to get a little worried but then again, I had to make myself realize that I have to quit doing so much worrying over petty things. I don't know what was wrong with my wife. She did not seem to be very receptive. Maybe it was just the kids on her nerves or maybe it was just me. I've not had a chance to search that out thoroughly in my mind yet. I went to my brother-in-law's van and got my aftershave and the kids were wild. Returned to the hospital and came back to my cell and began talking to my wife, and all of a sudden we were in an argument. I thought I came here to figure why I felt I had to have a drink. I feel I have that accomplished at this time, and my drinking problem dealt with (not cured because it will never be), but at least there was a solution rendered. I plan to get as much of the outside pressures off me as possible, get my family reunited again at whatever cost, and just become me once again. But all of a sudden, my wife said I was thinking I was well just after two weeks, and I had way too many issues that could not be resolved in just two weeks. I also have not figured that one out because for the past year, all she has told me is that she wanted me to stop drinking. I thought everything would be

Chapter 10

okay. Well, I've quit the drinking so help me God, and now I'm back out in left field. She stated she would not continue to live like we had, and it was up to me to figure out why I went crazy all the time. She was through with it all. She was tired of me threatening to kill her and myself. I had no idea what she was talking about. What the hell does she think she married? She said I had caused too many problems for her and the kids and her family and mine. I assume her family knows I no longer drink and that I've received medical help. I will apologize to her younger sister (for that is all I owe an apology to) then they should accept me as a whole person again. For some reason she has this guilt feeling that I can't seem to break through. I try talking to her, opening up my feelings with her, and I am rejected. I don't know what to do. I really felt I had things under control, and now I am not sure. She wanted me get medical help, I did, I feel so very strongly that I have this alcohol problem under control and will day by day assure and pray that I will never take another drink and remain sober from now on but all of a sudden she does not believe me. She states that she is not the sick person in this whole thing—I never said she was. All I want is to be reunited with my family, and if this requires a job change then I see no problem with that. Less than two weeks ago, she said she would help me. I came here to get help, feel good about finally being big enough to admit that I can't do it all. I need to relieve myself of some of these pressures, confide in her that I want her to have her life back again, and all hell breaks loose. I just don't understand what's going on. I try one thing and she

Chapter 10

rejects it. I try another (change location, job placement, whatever) to ease the pressures, and I still find myself out in left field. I know I have hurt her in the past— (I haven't but the alcohol in me has and I do dearly apologize for that) But that is in the past, it is gone. And tomorrow will be today before we know it. I tried once before to stop drinking on my own and did not accomplish it—maybe in her mind she can't let go of that defeat I experienced and does not trust me now. There are no guarantees to anything, whether one stays twenty-eight days, six days, twelve days, or a lifetime. All I can do is try to assure her that I will, by the grace of God, never take another drink and I must do this one day at a time. I received a homemade card from my daughter that stated "All I want Daddy is for you to be cheerful" and that "I love you." If that isn't enough to make a father quit a habit or addiction of any kind, then he should no longer be a father. I tried to explain to my wife tonight that I want a unified family again, and I could not break the ice. I know I have done so many wrongs in this past year or so, but I am not going to let myself get hung up on this "guilt" kick. I am looking at tomorrow and growing today for tomorrow. What is past is past and if I could cut my right arm off to change that, I would but I can't change yesterday, I can only change today and look forward to tomorrow. I know that I have accomplished the goal of stopping the abuse of alcohol right now. I feel I am wasting my time locked up in this ward—that I could do much more good just being with my family, showing, no, proving to them that daddy doesn't have to drink anymore. I could spend the next two weeks with

Chapter 10

nobody but them and heal many relations which I have lost just by being me once again. Instead, I have to sit here twenty-four hours a day going absolutely crazy while they are being carted all over the country wondering what is happening to dad. If only my wife would understand that it is me once again. And forever, then maybe I would have a chance to maintain sanity and mend a lot of ill feelings. Right now I am at a loss for answers but maybe through prayer and conversation with her we can work things out. I know we both need counseling. I know she is not to be at blame for it was my drinking that got us in this mess to begin with—but I do know she is very stubborn and has some problems in dealing with what I have done in the past. I will try hard to understand this and try even harder to come to some solution, but it is going to take time. I am wasting my time here and this I can attest to as a fact. I was not a chronic alcoholic or addict as they have here most of the time. And it does not take the same amount of time for everybody to learn how to stay away from an addiction. I'm tired, bored, and pissed off because I, in my mind, had at least come to some solutions which lifted a tremendous amount of weight off me, and now it is all blown to hell. It's 2:37 a.m., and I'm going to bed.

4/13/1984 My journal

We finally had a big fight tonight. I just couldn't keep my mouth shut any longer. I don't remember exactly how it started, but I do feel bad. I am sure he didn't need that on top of everything else. I am just tired of having to pretend that everything

Chapter 10

is okay, and that I am his dutiful wife. He was telling me about what he feels is the problem and what solutions he has come up with. It is the same old thing. Let's change careers and jobs and move to a new city and then everything will be okay. He wants to become a pilot. That is what we have done over and over. I have been carrying so much anger for a long time. I usually can hold it in, but I am just tired of hearing how it is all about him when he does not care enough about his family to try to figure out what is really going on. He just complains about everything and is not willing to put any effort into his counseling opportunities or doing anything that might help him begin a real recovery process. He is just playing games and manipulating again. It is the same old story. When I brought up all of his attempts to kill me and himself with the guns, he acted like he had no idea what I was talking about. I was furious. I am just tired of all his game playing.

The kids were here and have played a lot. My oldest son cried when we drove away. He felt bad that we were leaving Keith there. I don't know how the kids can stand any of this either. We have uprooted them from their lives because of him, and he tries to manipulate them, too. I am so angry with him and have been for many years.

4/14/84 Keith's journal

1:00 a.m.

Had a pretty good day today—Folks came and brought the camper. My kids were here, and we were all a family again

Chapter 10

with me, my wife and kids—although in a different environment. My wife and I met with the psychologist for a rather long session, and I feel that we made great progress, although we have a long way to go. I feel we need time alone to learn each other's "new" way of life. The psychologist feels the same and is going to try to have me on outpatient care for approximately ten days under her care so we may seek help if need be. This will take place of the ten-day aftercare program. But my wife kept saying that we did not need marriage counseling right now. The problem was my insane behavior. The psychologist tried to explain to her that it all had to do with the alcohol issue. She also suggested that my wife and I need a few days with just the kids in our home environment, so the children can also make similar adjustments. My wife still did not agree. I don't know what is wrong with her. It seems like she is trying to make this not work. I really think this is an excellent idea especially for the kids. They have been pulled from their school, entered in another, and to be put back in their old environment is going to be hard on them. They need time also to learn their new dad, for even if I have only drank heavy a short period of time, in little kids minds they forget quickly but yet learn fast. They now need to forget the drunken father and relearn their real dad. I believe this holds true for her, as my wife, and myself, as her husband. We are going to have to rediscover one another in many ways for both of us must make both changes and sacrifices. Can we do this on our own, pushed back in the same environment and many hundreds of miles away from the hospital?

Chapter 10

I feel a little hesitant to try, and it seems very logical to me for me to become an outpatient and for us to have time of our own with the psychologist close by just in case we need her. I really think she is excellent, and I can't believe how she can perceive both mine and my wife's thoughts as she does. I would really feel much more comfortable having her close during this initial learning stage that we both must go through. I feel I have the problem of alcohol defeated (with God's help and understanding it is one day at a time for the rest of my life), but I also know that since I no longer drink, I am a different man, my wife is going to react in a different manner and she must become a different woman. I wish she could see this. We need this time together! Must go, She will be here early tomorrow for I get some time away from this place so must be ready by 8:00. I felt more like a productive human being today than I have in many, many days. END 1:41 a.m. PS Hope to feel even more like one tomorrow—we'll see?

4/14/1984 My journal

I felt better tonight. Keith and I met with the psychologist today. We talked about my anger, and she said it came from all the changes. I tried to tell her what our life outside the hospital had been like, the murder and suicide attempts, but she just ignored it. I think she thinks that I am just making up stuff. She insists that what we need is marriage counseling. I am ready to give up. It has been almost two weeks, and I see no progress. Keith is still complaining about everything and acting like he already knows it all. He

Chapter 10

says that after two weeks, he has worked through his alcohol problem. What about the shooting his wife and self problem? Somehow he has forgotten all the horrors that I have lived with for the last decade. I am trying hard not to hate him. The psychologist had us make a list of what we liked about each other. I told her at this point in our relationship I could not make that list. She told me to go back to why I married him. I just wish that we were really making progress in this mess. I am just ready to be back with my kids all the time.

4/15/1984 Keith's journal

Sunday

Had a pretty good day today. My wife came around 8:15 a.m., and I was able to spend most of the day with her until about 8:30 p.m. this evening. (Only 4 hours out of the place of course—that's all they allow). We played some golf at the driving range, had an average lunch, and did some other things, and then it was already almost past time to return to the cell. We spent the rest of the time here at the hospital. Not much really to say tonight except really the day was only half good because I was subconsciously thinking of having to return to this place. My wife acted different, but I think she is as tired of this place as I am. I think I will get much more out of this, If that is possible, with the exception of the psychologist, when I go to out-patient care. God, if only it would be tomorrow. I'm going to try to go to bed earlier tonight and do some reading and see if I can relax that way. It is now only 12:20 a.m. and I'm going

Chapter 10

to quit with this last thought to be put on paper. They say to quit drinking one must think in terms of "one day at a time," but to survive through this ordeal—it takes every ounce of self-discipline "one hour at a time." END 12:29 a.m.

4/15/1984 My journal

Keith had time out of the clinic today. We hit balls at the golf course and then ate lunch out. His sister and her husband came up to visit. I like them so much. They helped me forget all the misery while they were here. Keith puts on a front for them, so he is more tolerable. I am going to his mom and dad's house for the night. I need to be with my kids.

4/16/1984 Keith's journal

12:10 a.m. Well, had an extremely boring day today. First session began at 9:00 a.m. It began with "barriers of staying sober." They listed physical, emotional, stability, gunny-sacking, and some others. Only problem is they didn't really know what any of them meant. I basically had to explain, and then they would come up with examples to give to the group. Then came the lovers and romantics crap—I sat there for two hours and listened to "suppose this," "suppose that," and, "what if". Let's get to the facts and educable literature and reality. One can only listen to speculating and hypothesizing so long. The trainees that tried to conduct the class are not professional on any basis and do not really know what they are reading from the loose-leaf book

Chapter 10

which was given to them twenty minutes earlier. I am so tired of being locked in this place just to listen to an x-junkie or alcoholic repeat over and over and over and over the same experiences or the same rehash that I have taught for years (not learned to live although I have now). But it just gets old. For instance, one monitor stated there were three things (something like that. I can't remember what she called them) but anyway she started naming (1) you are what you are, (2) you are what others think you are, and so on, ad infinitum. Well, actually, she was giving us the answers to the personality traits of all individuals, and there happens to be four of them, not three. The one she did not give the class is probably one of the most important as related to the alcoholic. I did not say anything. I did not correct or do anything, but it was all

I could muster to not ask if I could teach the lesson. Crap like that is really about to get to me. After all this —do nothing, know nothing, the BS they gave us— we got an hour-and-a-half discussion and a poor quality film on all the reasons one should not quit early. Stay the full twenty-eight days and receive all this wisdom. I have not yet (with the exception of the psychologist) received one bit of intelligent, well planned piece of informative education on alcoholism. What I have done has been through my own decision-making process and getting back in touch with God and with reality. I'm tired of thinking about it twenty-four hours a day. I am locked in this place and for what? I'm just sick and tired of having to sit and listen to this "common sense" crap when I'm paying $6,000.00 for, quote, "professional help," end quote. I feel as if I'll go

Chapter 10

crazy if something is not done and done soon. Forget that crap. Let's get to something worthwhile. I played twelve games of solitaire today—beat him only once. I went to PT and exercised with bar bells. I saw my wife very little; we met about thirty minutes for lunch and then a couple hours tonight. She is going through hell also. But she doesn't have to put up with what I do, and I can sense that she is getting her fill of it. She just keeps acting like she doesn't trust me. I don't know which one will have a nervous breakdown first—she or me. For some reason I am feeling she is not really wanting to stay here any longer, and that she is getting tired of coming to this place for a thirty-minute or two-hour visit every day. She doesn't even think about how hard it is for me. I don't know what to do. If only they would understand and let me be outpa-

tient as soon as possible, then I think we could work things out because we then could talk things over on a one-to-one basis and maybe not destroy anything further. I can't blame her though. She has been jerked away from her children, her home, and can't even see her husband when she wants, even though I feel sincere about my having this alcohol thing under control. I am seriously considering checking myself out of here whether they allow me outpatient care or not. I can't decide which is doing the most harm— my staying here and absolutely going bongos (along with my wife) or checking out and (with the understanding that I will try to never drink ever in my life again— and really knowing this) just checking it to them.

Chapter 10

God, please help me come to some conclusion. If this place were professional and organized, regarding in some educational aspect, it would be okay. By the way, guess what we went over today? We are now almost two weeks into the program. We discussed the rules and guidelines of patients in ATC. That is, "you'll not leave the hospital," "you'll sign out, and so on. Now tell me about organized rehabilitation programs. This is ridiculous. I'm up to almost three packs of cigarettes a day now. If the boredom and ignorance around here don't kill me, the lung cancer will. My wife and I talked to the psychologist tonight, and she wants us to meet tomorrow. I may bring some of this up to her. I am just confused right now and don't really know what to do. I have prayed and prayed for some help in making a decision. And I am get-

ting this stronger and stronger feeling that staying here is doing more harm to me, my family, and my mind. I've even lost count of days. I don't even remember if this day 8 or 9 or 10 or 11—or what since I supposedly came from what they call first step. It's like prison—in fact, it is worse because you have to meet all day and listen to this elementary garbage. At least in prison you can play ball, pool, and so on. I think I'm going crazy. I am depressed.

The psychologist wants a list of all the good things I see in my wife by the time of our meeting tomorrow, so I must stop and do that. I hope to maintain my sanity through God's help and understanding. END—12:57 a.m. PS our car was sideswiped tonight on the left side. My wife and kids just left.

Chapter 10

4/16/1984 My journal

I had lunch with Keith today. He was, as usual, complaining about a session he had today. He felt that the two teachers were unprofessional and that he had wasted his time. He was concerned that the instructors had ignored a dream that one of the clients had. I think he just focuses on any other problem around him so he doesn't have to dig into what is wrong with him. I did not see him much today—just from 8:00 to 10:00. We talked a little, and then a nurse interrupted us to ask if we knew the rules to 42. So we played 42 until I had to leave. It was better than having to hear him complain about everything. He told me that he thought I was getting tired of the whole thing. He has no clue how tired I am of living like we have lived for the last decade and more. I would have already been gone if I could only get the kids and I away from him safely and know he would leave us alone. I feel so trapped and angry. I got out to the car and found that somebody had hit it. What a way to end the day.

4/17/1984 Keith's journal

11:15 p.m. Today was a little better, although I can feel myself getting deeper and deeper into a psychotic depression about why I started drinking. Yes, I've been told why most all people start drinking or using alcohol as a scapegoat but I'm not all people nor am I paying for all people. I need to know why I, me, Keith, used it. It is not a chemical addiction problem because it does not bother me to not drink, or if I do, I can become sober without a drink or DTs or whatever.

Chapter 10

(I don't know what DTs are but I have heard of them). I know this for a fact. I am not saying that I'm not an alcoholic for I am because I have abused it before (this past year). And I would probably do it again if I allowed myself to have a drink. I hope to never do that again, and with God's help, I feel very confident in that regard. I also feel like the inside of me is about to jump clear out. I am a hyperactive person to begin with. I have certain goals, challenges, and areas of growth in life that I want to achieve but not achieve at any cost or risk. I can do without them, but I am not going to just lay back, be dormant, and let the world go by. I am not put together this way. I feel as if I am a young colt, and somebody is trying to cold break me. Today while talking with the psychologist, I received a flash, (actually the psychologist was talking to my

wife and I was listening), I got a picture or image of me breaking a colt last year. It is like they (all of them, even my wife) are trying to break my mental spirit and drive and then tell me what is wrong and try to build upon that broken person or personality or whatever. I see in my mind that I want a flow chart with the achievement line going up and they want a straight line with no feeling, no initiative, or drive. I will not or cannot allow this to happen to me. One has absolutely no freedom of choice, no opportunity to make self decisions, or anything. That may be all and well for the person who has been drinking for thirty years and has been drunk twenty of them. One can't treat half-dozen medical problems all exactly the same way. We are not a herd of cattle. We are individuals and need individual and personalized help. I know this sounds crazy, even

Chapter 10

to me, but I swear I have the feeling that "if we can break him down to our level and feed him some elementary psychology BS then he will feel as if the program is good. "Crap—I know as much psychology as anybody here, and I probably know just enough to get myself in trouble. I know that I worry about tomorrow and probably the next day and all of today, and that I am a people pleaser. And that I hold in a lot of tension and emotions. And this is probably why I resorted (or my excuse to resort) to drinking. But my question and the primary reason I came here is to find out why. All people do these things to an extent and cope with them, but I let it run my life so to speak. And I need to know why. That's why I decided to spend the $6,000.00-plus on this, and I've received absolutely nothing. The psychologist has *helped my wife and I understand each other's feelings better and given us ways to communicate more freely. BUT we could have done that with a marriage psychologist for one tenth of the money. I want help on why I felt the need to resort to the bottle and answers as to how to correct this feeling. Yes, this place has proven to me one thing. I doubt I will ever (I hope not to) take another drink as long as I live because I never want to endure such a traumatic experience again. It has given me that determination. But that does not relieve the tension I have with my wife. She keeps thinking I am not changing. It's like she thinks I am so bad that I can't change. I need ways or answers or whatever it takes to just relax, take one thing at a time, and not feel so nervous, and tense. I feel like my life is upside down. If I could do this then there*

Chapter 10

would be no doubt about my drinking problem. I feel I have more of a psychological problem than drinking problem but used alcohol to relieve the tension, or at least numb it. I know that is not the way. There are much more lucrative ways of handling one's tensions or nervousness or whatever it is. All the family on my mother's side was this way, very nervous, always on edge, although they never used alcohol. I did. And yes, I regret it for I feel I could and should have gotten help for my downs last year prior to starting drinking so heavily. I'm sorry I didn't, but one can't dwell on the past (if only she would see that). I want to look to the future and see a different future for me, but I will assure you this place isn't getting me anywhere. All I hear is a repetition of something I already know, and I realize it sounds as though I "think I know it all and they can't help me no matter what," but that's the God's truth. I have had nothing thus far to actually help with my initial problem. If my wife or I either one make any comment or statement to the effect that I have had this problem, (not drinking problem) probably all my life and we would like to know or try to figure it out, we get a "cold shoulder" or "change the subject type attitude" response with no answer, I am not chemically dependent on alcohol such as the drug addict or thirty- or forty-year drinker. I hold all this frustration inside of me, and all I need to do is figure out a way to release this or not even get it. There would be no problem with my drinking habits. (I just turned on a Beethoven violin concerto—sounds peaceful and relaxing). Anyway, my being locked in here for chronic alcoholism is not the answer. I don't care

Chapter 10

what the counselors say about "thinking we are cured or whatever else." I know that I am regressing and becoming very depressed, and that is not good at all. I have participated in all the sessions and everything they have asked right down to the T, but have received nothing. Tomorrow will be two weeks. I think and I feel as if I am about to explode. I made the comment in my thoughts on paper last night that I don't know who is going to have the nervous breakdown first—me or my wife. I really meant that from the bottom of my heart because I feel I am fixing to fall apart if something isn't done. Anyway, the psychologist just kind of laughed it off (and I am not blaming her), but she thought I was just making a joke or pun or something. I'm dead serious that if I have to remain incarcerated in this place one more night, I may go off *the deep end. If I were getting specific help for my specific problem and some answers or at least suggestions as to how to correct them then I could handle it. But all I receive are in-group sessions over and over and over on each of the patients telling why they thought they drank, how they got started, why they came here. Then we might have a supposed lecture on schizophrenia or paranoia that I could—and have—received in a $60.00 college class. I think I will absolutely go crazy. I think maybe I am going crazy; I've never sat down and listened to Beethoven before in my life or wrote a daily summary like this. I feel that I can't talk to the wall or they may put me in the ha-ha farm, but I can record my feelings and thoughts on paper and at least release some of the frustrations and anxieties I receive from this place each day.*

Chapter 10

Our session today with the psychologist was a kind of "watch out Keith, here it comes." I picked up on that, but for some reason my wife didn't. The psychologist is trying, and I do not mean to put her down or be critical, but she said some things today I just can't accept. For instance, she said I am too dependent on my wife. We are husband and wife and should be dependent on one another, and at the same time still have our own person to deal with. We know that and do a pretty good job at it. I will admit we do almost everything together and with the children but we are, in that manner, closer to one another than most couples and enjoy doing things together. I see no wrong with our marital relationships here. Our circle of husband and wife, mother and father, just overlap a little farther than the average. Anyway, she (the psycholo-

gist) said more things I just can't agree with such as me being too much the controller of the family. They are my family, and I will provide, love, and protect—even if it is a mother hen situation—to the utmost of my ability and capability. I strongly believe in this.

Well, it is way past one o'clock, and my brain is getting tired of recapitulating the day's events because I am beginning to forget what transpired. I leave with this one last statement, or prayer, if you (I) choose, "Please God, give me the power and courage to endure one more day and I will try to take it one hour at a time and turn it over to you, for you are the only one that can help me maintain my sanity and self-control to not just blow completely up. PS If I don't get some straight answers from these people, I will

Chapter 10

be checking out soon. I am not an ignorant person nor am I the smartest by any means, but I know I am regressing rather than advancing. By the way, I have plenty of people who will verify that none of us has received anything from this mess except the absolute determination that we will never return. 1:54 a.m. END

4/17/1984 My journal

Today has been a bad day. I got up this morning and cleaned up the camper, bathed and dressed and went to town. I stopped and left my glasses to be fixed. Then I checked at the nursing home to see if I could volunteer some while I am here. I am so tired of being away from my children. I don't know why I am here as I know now that this is not going to work with Keith, either. He lies and refuses to take any responsibility for what he has become. I stopped at Wal-Mart to look for Easter clothes for the kids. I found a pair of shoes for our daughter but didn't buy them as she likes to pick things out herself now. I met Keith in the cafeteria at 12:30. He ate lunch. I'd already eaten so I just sat and drank a coke. We were supposed to meet the psychologist at 1:00. We went upstairs to find her, and she wasn't there so we just went back to his room. He read aloud to me from his daily journal. The psychologist walked in while he was reading and sat and listened to him. The session lasted until 4:00. I am concerned—worried a lot—that Keith's problems are being bypassed, and all of the counseling is focused on our marriage relationship. How strong can a relationship be if having a gun held to my head every night is about all the interaction we

Chapter 10

have. I have tried to tell her but she just moves on to another topic. She keeps focusing on our need for counseling for marital problems. I did not feel good about our session. Keith thinks she is great and that she is really helping. Of course, he does. He does not have to face any of his issues. I felt that she was just pacifying me with her answers. I think she has decided that I exaggerate about our life. I am sure that Keith tells her this, too. He still is focused on getting out. All he does is complain. He is so selfish and thinks only of himself. All he does is manipulate everybody. I am so tired of it all.

4/18/1984 Keith's journal

12:08 p.m. Well, not much happened today—had a bunch of terms read to us from a sheet of paper. This took about an hour then one of the counselors got up and told us about problem-solving techniques, which I have taught and used for over ten years. I'm not saying that his presentation was worthless, but I knew everything that he was teaching. In fact, he made a couple of assumptions that really were not correct.

I feel pretty good (although still uptight and lonely) but pretty good because I am checking out tomorrow and going under the care of a psychiatric MD, which will help me get to the root of the problem. And I will be away from this nerve-racking, petty bull. Oh, one of the counselor's words of advice today were "stop _____ on yourself or don't ____ on yourself attitude." Now he may be able to pull that on some of the recovering alcoholics in there, but that is not what I con-

Chapter 10

sider teachable techniques. I'm sorry but I can't put up with type of techniques and lecture any more. Especially when it is not all facts and a lot of personal feelings are implemented when they do not even pertain to the subject, which is being discussed. I never dreamed a medical institution that is well advertised (falsely) could be run so unorganized, non-structured, and elementary. The psychiatric MD was supposed to come by tonight but he did not make it. He must have gotten held up somewhere but he will be by tomorrow morning—early I hope. I feel good about the decision that I have made. I told my wife and all hell broke loose. I know she is not happy about it, but she has no idea how bad it is here. She will get used to it when she sees how I have changed. I feel now that I can get to the root of my problem which really is not alcohol, but something within me churning all the time, all tied up inside. And like I can't stand it here one more minute. I know what a lot of the problem is, and it is that I know I need better professional help than this place can offer. I have, I think, come to the realization of what caused the bottle, but I want and need to know why I'm that way and how to work to overcome it. I want to know the steps necessary to take to keep myself relaxed inside and out and not on pins and needles most of the time. I really feel this doctor can help with this, and then I can follow up with it at home. Maybe this doctor could recommend somebody that is good and I can trust.

This afternoon all I did was play solitaire (kind of expensive solitaire at these prices), but I get as much out of that as

Chapter 10

I would have a group session or lecture. It sounds like I'm taking that "I know it all" attitude, but I'm just telling the plain truth. I have learned all of this in college and have also taught all these things. They say that with group discussions you should get something more from others' experience, but one can only get so much from the same four people, hearing the same thing over and over. There is only so much to tell about one's self. Well, it is after 1:00 a.m. I think I will shower and clean up so I won't have to in the morning. Maybe that will relax me some. There is a lot more I would like to think about but I must also watch the time. I'm getting very little rest in this place as it is—on average about three to four hours a night. This is not sufficient to support the mental anguish that I go through every day, and I'm really beginning to feel it. I'm getting more and more hypercritical and withdrawn, and that is not good. I hope to God I am gone tomorrow by 10:00 or 10:30 a.m. END 1:28 a.m.

4/18/1984 My journal

I slept very little last night. I am so upset that Keith is going to leave the program. I have tried so hard to get someone to listen to me—to understand how crazy and dangerous his day-to-day behavior has been for the last thirteen years. I can't get anyone to hear what I am saying. They think I am just exaggerating the alcoholism issue. I have told them that it is a life-and-death issue. I do not feel that they have addressed any of his real issues. He has been able to manipulate the whole staff, including the counselors, the psychologist, and his

Chapter 10

parents. He manipulates everybody and is just used to always having his way. He keeps talking about the psychiatric MD agreeing with what he is doing but so far, this doctor has not spent time with him. I asked Keith not to check out of the program until he talks with him. But if the doctor doesn't come to the hospital when Keith says he should, then Keith feels he can't stand to wait. He thinks his way is the only way. I am so tired of having to live this life. Why can't I get help? I know he is going to end up killing himself and me if somebody doesn't listen to what is happening at home. I just can't handle living with him anymore, but I don't see how I can get out safely. This was my final hope so now I don't know what will happen. Maybe I can get his mom and dad to listen to me and help us. I am scared of what is coming.

As I read over Keith's journal entries, I found it interesting that he never talked about his real problem. His secret remained hidden, possibly even to him. He made several comments in his journals that made me wonder about multiple personalities or possession again. He acted like he did not remember all of the times he attempted suicide and tried to shoot me. He also started believing that he had chosen to come to this center to get help. He did not remember that he was forced to come out of desperation by his mom and dad and me.

I wondered if he had grown so hardened to the truth over the years that it no longer seemed real to him, and he could not face it. He never focused on why he was in the program. He spent most of his hours complaining and looking for reasons why he did not have a problem and did not need to be there.

After Keith left the hospital he planned to return to his old job as a high school adminis-

Chapter 10

trator, but his boss informed him that his doctor had notified the school board that he did not complete the treatment program. He was told that he could not return to work until he completed another thirty-day treatment program. The kids and I went through another month of agony having to drive back and forth to another hospital, but at least we were back at home. It was much easier for the kids as they returned to their old routine.

Keith completed this program and returned to work. Most of the people he worked with were thrilled to have him back. They truly felt that he was the best administrator that they had ever worked with. He definitely had a lot of charisma and I am sure that he was an excellent administrator. I still find it difficult to understand how he could function so well at work and become a psychotic mess at home.

Chapter 11

ಖಂ
For I know the thoughts that I think toward you,
saith the LORD, thoughts of peace, and not of
evil, to give you an expected end.
Jeremiah 29:11

Keith stayed sober for a month. Then he started sneaking around, drinking and hiding his alcohol. It was much worse this time. I found it hidden in every room of the house, in the shed, the garage, and even under the house. I could not understand it. Keith had been through two programs and had more support than most recovering alcoholics at home, at work, and in the community. Still, I knew that we had not

Chapter 11

reached the core of the problem. I felt like the alcohol was just a symptom. I knew that there was more happening than could be attributed to alcoholism. He was filled with rage, and I always wondered what created the deep anger inside of him.

Our lives were headed downhill again when Keith suddenly decided that he wanted to move closer to his parents. I expect that something happened at work, and he was called on it. Or maybe he lost his sense of self-value now that people knew he had a weakness. He wrote a resignation letter, and I gave two-week's notice at the bank where I worked. We called a realtor and put our house up for sale. Keith's sister owned a house that was vacant, and we planned to rent it. I started boxing up our things.

Three days later I came home from work, and Keith was already home. He had been drinking and was pacing the floor. He was extremely agitated. He suddenly stopped in front of me and told me that he was going to move everything we had that night. I knew that this was impossible as I had not finished packing everything and I still had over a week to work. He ignored me and hooked up the flatbed trailer to the pickup and started loading the furniture. He got the pickup and the trailer loaded and left. He did not say a word to me or the kids. He just drove off. It was already after 6:00 p.m., and he drove 350 miles, unloaded the vehicles and headed back home. He returned to the house about 2:00 a.m. and loaded up again and took off. This time he took everything. There was nothing left in the house except the telephone, a suitcase I had packed for the kids and me, and our blankets and pillows. We had no food and no beds. We literally were left in an empty house. I made it a game for the kids as we camped out in the den near the wood stove. But my mind swirled with this new insanity.

Chapter 11

The next morning I took the kids to school and drove into town to the bank where I worked. I picked up my check which was around $200.00 and thanked the Lord that he had provided for our food and gas to make the trip. I explained to my boss that I was not going to be able to work the full two weeks and that we were heading out of town that day. I scheduled to have the telephone and electricity shut off at the end of the week and cleaned the house as best I could without any tools.

I loaded our blankets, pillows, and suitcase into the car and drove to the school to pick up the kids. I checked them out of school, and we headed out of town. We had gone about five miles down the highway when the car started to hiss. I turned around and went back to the house. I called Keith and told him our situation. He told me that there was nothing wrong with the car and that we needed to drive on down. I got back on the highway and went a couple of miles and the car kept cutting out, so I turned around and drove to the shop. I talked with the mechanic, and he told me that I needed to leave the car with them but he didn't have anyone that could take us home. I drove the children home and unloaded our stuff. At this time, they were five, seven, and ten years old. I locked them in the house and told them I would be right back. I dropped off the car at the shop and told them to call me when it was ready. I walked back to the house. The mechanic took two days to fix the car, and the kids and I were stranded in an empty house. We did walk to the grocery store which was about 2 miles from the house, but otherwise we just kept to ourselves. I was tired of explaining to others about our problems. It did not seem to make anything better.

When the car was ready it cost $170.00 so we were able to pay the bill and get on the road. It was late afternoon by the time we left, and we didn't reach the house we were renting until

Chapter 11

10:00 p.m. As we drove up, there were several cars parked out front. Keith's parents and both his sisters were there. His sister's pastor was also with them. As we came in the door, I asked them where Keith was and someone said that he was drunk and ran into the bathroom when he saw us drive up. The bathroom door was locked so I ran outside just as he was crawling out the bathroom window. Everyone raced out to the front yard with shock on their faces. He jumped in the pickup and started backing out of the driveway. I was close enough to jump in and turn off the keys. I took them out and got out of the pickup. Keith went into a rage and yelled and cursed me. I turned around and went back into the house where my children waited, leaving his family to deal with him. So our new start immediately became the same old behavior that we had struggled with for years. But at least, this time, his family had witnessed a tiny part of what I had dealt with for years.

During this time, his family and I were able to convince Keith that he needed to see a psychiatrist and talk to someone who could really help him understand what was going on in his head. He had always become so angry whenever I broached the subject before, but I think he felt that he was at the bottom now. He had lost his dream job and was now back to substitute teaching, and living in a small house that belonged to his sister. He had lost almost everything. Of course, he insisted on seeing the doctor alone, so I do not know how honest he was about his life. The psychiatrist diagnosed him as bipolar and gave him a prescription for medication.

Once again, there a small ray of hope shining through. But it wasn't long before I realized that he was not taking any of his medication. In order to safely take the medication, he had to stop drinking, and he chose to continue drinking.

Chapter 12

ಸಂಯ
"For the LORD your God is he that goes with you, to fight for you against your enemies, to save you."
Deuteronomy 20:4

*E*ven with all the weeks spent in rehab treatment, the medications that had been prescribed for Keith, and the many doctors he had seen, there was still so much confusion in our lives. There were more questions now than ever. No matter how hard I searched for the answers, I found none. I know now that God had a reason to keep me in the dark, although I still do not totally understand. In His time, He would open up the truth to me and then I would be set free. But it was still a long time before that would come.

It wasn't long before our lives were right back where they had been before Keith had gone into either one of the rehabilitation centers. He continued to drink and almost every evening would race through the house in an uncontrollable rage. But now he only brought the guns out two or three nights a week. I was thankful for that.

Evenings were our worst times. He would start drinking early in the day and by suppertime, he was always drunk. The only thing predictable about his behavior was that he was unpredictable and always so full of anger.

It was odd how quickly his behavior could change in the middle of a tirade when he was interrupted. If the telephone rang or one of the children got out of bed, he would become quiet. His voice and actions would change so drastically when he answered the phone, that I

Chapter 12

thought I must be dreaming. If someone came to the door, he would offer them coffee or a drink. He would sit and talk to them as though nothing unusual had been happening. These sudden changes made me wonder if I was going crazy. As soon as the company left or the child was back in bed, he would pick up right where he left off as though there had been no interruptions.

There was no escaping his anger. If I tried to go to bed, he would follow me to the bedroom, and now his outbursts were becoming increasingly violent. The children's bedrooms were next to ours so I did my best to keep him away from them. If I attempted to defend myself, his conversation and his behavior would become so confusing that before long nothing he did or said would make any sense, and his actions towards me would become more dangerous. I soon found that the safest thing for me to do was to just listen to him without speaking a word.

Many nights I asked God how much longer He was going to let this go on. But there was never an answer; although, in the midst of the worst of these situations, He would grant me such peace. I realized that I no longer was afraid and I knew that God was with me. I knew that He had not forsaken us. He would change things in His time. I just had to be patient and rely totally on Him. I only hoped and prayed that this race would soon be finished.

The kids enrolled in school and our lives returned to somewhat of a routine. With all of Keith's problems, I never thought that he would ever be able to work and support us again. I knew that the time was coming that I would have to be the breadwinner. I decided to go back to college and complete the requirements for my teaching degree.

We had a savings account and had finally sold our house up north, so we had finances to keep us stable until I could teach full time. We

Chapter 12

both signed up to substitute teach and usually worked two to three days a week. We did not have any additional bills other than rent, food, and utilities, so we did not have financial problems to worry about.

In the eye of the storm, I found times of peace and serenity. We would walk the kids to school each morning and then sometimes go out for breakfast. Keith was not as stressed as he had been when he was working full time. We did have occasions when we found pleasure in what we were doing. But I knew that even though there were times that things were quiet on the outside, underneath a violent storm still raged.

I enrolled in school and was enjoying my return to college. It had been a long time since I had been able to accomplish something on my own. I discovered that I was really pretty bright! I loved learning and really enjoyed the friendships that I developed at school. But it wasn't long before Keith began to resent my new life. He would question me about everything and developed paranoia about any friendships I had. If a professor wrote a positive note on any of my work, he would read it entirely out of context.

I worked hard in all my classes and often spent time working on papers and projects, but I never neglected my children or my household duties. I sometimes did not get much sleep, but I knew that I had obligations to be there for the kids. No matter how hard I worked to keep things in balance, Keith resented everything about my schooling. But I knew that I was doing what I had to do. I was working towards a better future for the kids. I knew that I had to stay on track and prepare myself to care for them. I was also discovering that I had the power to do something positive with my life. I did not know how things would work out for us but I knew that I had to stay the course regardless of how Keith felt about it or how much rage it caused.

Chapter 12

A few weeks after I started attending classes, we had already gone to bed when Keith suddenly jumped out of bed in a rage. He packed a bag and left in our motor home without any explanation. He called me about four hours later wanting me to come to get him out of jail in a town about 150 miles away. He had totaled our motor home and was being charged with a DUI. I told him that I was not about to rouse the kids and come to rescue him from something he caused. He went crazy over the phone, but this time, I had a choice. I hung up. About thirty minutes later, his mother called me and told me that they were going to go and get him. I asked her to take him home with them and let us have a peaceful night.

Chapter 13

ಬಂಡ
"Peace I leave with you, my peace I give
unto you: not as the world gives, give
I unto you. Let not your heart be
troubled, neither let it be afraid."
John 14:27

*T*he day came when Keith found an ad in the paper for a job that he was interested in. A school district in a small community in the mountains needed a principal. He immediately sent in his application and his resume. They were very interested in him and called him in for an interview. The superintendent also called Keith's previous boss and had a long conversa-

Chapter 13

tion with him. He was aware of Keith's drinking problems before he met Keith. After interviewing him, the school district called and offered Keith the job. We prepared to move again.

Keith was so excited. He had another chance to prove himself. I believed that this job would either restore our lives or destroy us. I knew that God had given Keith another chance to get his life straightened out.

I talked with my children and asked them not to ask to go with their father when we went somewhere and took both cars. I knew they were aware of their father's chaotic behavior but, as children, they didn't understand the dangers of being alone with him. I tried my best to make them understand how important it was that they remember this.

The little mountain community had a reception to welcome their new principal. It was a beautiful place, and everyone we met seemed to be very friendly. Everything seemed so perfect. But that feeling didn't last long. It was soon replaced with a feeling of apprehension.

We purchased a home that was surrounded by mountains and near a river. We drove up one afternoon for a get-together for the community to meet their new principal. Keith drove his pickup because he was going to go early and spend some time at the school. The kids and I drove up later to meet our new neighbors. When we arrived we found that alcohol was being served and Keith had been drinking. When it was time to go home, I called the kids to come with me. The boys wanted to stay with their dad. I struggled, not knowing how to handle this situation. People were still visiting with Keith and I knew I could not make a scene. I tried to talk them into going with me but they wouldn't budge, and Keith finally told me to leave them alone. He would bring them home. Reluctantly, my daughter and I left. I prayed for their safety most of our way home.

Chapter 13

I waited anxiously at home. It was getting late and I thought they should have been home at least an hour before. I decided to drive down the highway and see if the truck had broken down. My daughter and I drove several miles out of town until I finally realized that the boys were in God's hands and I was powerless. I surrendered them into His care and we drove back home.

Shortly after we arrived, they drove up. Keith was really drunk but it seemed that the boys were okay. They came into the house, and I could tell that Keith was already angry. He wanted his supper so I warmed up tacos for them. He just went crazy. He grabbed the tacos and slammed them into the wall, turned around, and walked out the door. I heard his pickup start and drive away.

We were all glad he left. The boys told me that on the way home a state policeman pulled in behind Keith. He was not trying to pull him over but Keith reached under his seat and placed his .357 magnum on his lap. He was driving without a license as he lost it when he had the DUI in the motor home. I know that the Lord was watching over them as the policeman did not stop them. I am so thankful he didn't. Keith might have shot him. I took this time to forbid the boys to ask to ride with their father again regardless of where we were going. I think they understood this time.

Things continued to fall apart. I was still attending college and having to drive 150 miles one way every day to go to classes. I was determined to complete my degree as Keith was getting worse. I would get up at 3:00 in the morning, get myself ready and fix breakfast for the kids. I would leave the house at 4:00 and return home around 5:00 every evening. I would fix supper and then spend time with the kids. After the kids were in bed, I would do laundry, get clothes ready for the next day, fix lunches and clean up the house. I did not spend time at

Chapter 13

home doing any school work when Keith was home. He resented what I was doing so much that it would always set him off.

Every Wednesday evening I had a late class and would stay until 9:00 p.m. That meant that it was close to midnight before I got home. I could not leave the kids alone with Keith so I asked my mother-in-law to drive seventy miles to our house and take care of the kids until I got home. She was so gracious and wanted me to finish my studies. She was willing to step in and do this.

I would always call the house before I went to class as I had to check with her to see if she felt safe with Keith or if I needed to come home. One particular Wednesday when I called she told me that I needed to come right home. Keith was out of control. The irony of the situation was that I was usually the one who outraged him, but I was also the only one who seemed to be able to eventually calm him down. His mother said that he had a pair of scissors in his back pocket and she was terrified that he was going to stab her. He was incoherent and totally out of control. I told her she needed to call the police and I was on the way.

It took me less than two hours to get home, speeding every mile of the way. When I arrived I expected to see the police but there were no official vehicles. I entered quietly through the back door. I checked on the kids and they were already in their beds. I spent a minute with each one of them and reassured them that they were safe. Then I went into my bedroom and sat for a minute trying to hear what was being said. I didn't want Keith to know I was home until I knew what was happening. He was yelling and cursing, but I couldn't understand what he was saying to his parents. His mother had not called the police but instead had called my father-in-law and he had driven up.

I finally went into the living room, and Keith was in the dining room with his father. I walked

Chapter 13

into the room, and he turned around and saw me. He grabbed me and threw me to the floor. He became physically violent so quickly that his dad was caught off guard. His dad had injuries he had received in an automobile accident a few years before so he was having a difficult time trying to restrain Keith. His mother finally called the police. When Keith realized that the police were coming, he began to calm down.

When the officer arrived, it turned out that he knew Keith from working with him in the schools. He took him outside and talked with him for about an hour. They came back into the house, and the officer told me he needed to talk to me. We walked outside while Keith and his parents stayed in the house. He told me that Keith thought I was having an affair with one of my professors, and that was why he was so upset. I was speechless but managed to tell him that I didn't even say bad words and I sure wouldn't think of committing adultery.

Keith's fear of me having an affair was not the problem. Something else was going on, and I told him that Keith often held a gun to my head and vacillated between killing me and committing suicide. I stated that he had been through two rehab centers for alcoholism but I knew that his problem was much greater than alcoholism. I asked him to check and see if the state police had any official reports or records on Keith. I disclosed that Keith's behavior was becoming more and more violent at home, and I just could not get anyone to help us.

About that time my in-laws came out the door and said they were going home. The state policeman sat with Keith until he finally dozed off. The officer was a fine Christian man whose wife's father had been an alcoholic. He just assumed that the alcohol was the problem, and he was very sympathetic toward Keith. He made it a habit of spending time at our house almost every evening to make sure we were okay. I

Chapter 13

know that God used him to help us get through these difficult times, although I don't think he fully realized how great our problem was.

From that point on our lives became even harder and I was more afraid. I could not leave the children alone with Keith, even in the daytime.

One evening, Keith became so violent that his behavior escalated while the children were still awake. It was during this time, that he not only threatened me but also put the gun to our twelve-year-old daughter's head when she told him to leave me alone. I thought our deaths would be the next event in our crumbling lives.

Keith started attending church again with us after we moved to this mountain community. One Sunday evening after we got home from church, I was fixing a bedtime snack for the kids when he came charging out of the bedroom, cursing and yelling. He had the rifle in his hands and was waving it around. I immediately grabbed the kids and headed out the door. We made it to the car before he grabbed me and told me that we weren't going anywhere. He had the rifle aimed at the car so I quietly told the children to go back inside but to be ready to sneak out to the car when I told them. I took them back to the bedroom telling him they were getting their pajamas on and brushing their teeth. Keith sat down in the living room nurturing a drink with his rifle in his lap. I had the children go out the back door and told them to get in the car and lock the doors and not to open them until they saw I was the only one who could get in. I instructed my daughter to put the keys in the ignition so all I would have to do was get it started. I went back and sat down in the living room pretending that the kids were all tucked in bed.

My precious children did exactly as they were told. I know they had to be terribly frightened, but by now this was becoming a routine occurrence for all of us. Keith got up to mix himself another drink, and I took that moment to

Chapter 13

race out the back door. The kids unlocked the door, and I slid in beside them. I started the car just as he reached us. He pointed the rifle at my window. I pushed the kids down on the floor and told them not to get up. I got out of the car and he told the kids to get out. He still had the rifle pointed at the car. I shook my head at them and told them to stay where they were. I knew I had to do something. I decided to try to get the rifle away from him and threw myself under it pushed it up. I got hold of it, but he still had it, too. We struggled and the rifle went off while it was pointed straight up. The impact threw Keith back and he fell on the ground. I jumped into the car, started it, put it into gear, and pulled forward. But Keith had gotten up off the ground and moved in front of us. He took the rifle butt and bashed out both headlights. It was close to midnight by now and we lived off a very busy highway. I knew I didn't have a choice and peeled out forcing him to move out from the front of the car. He lost his balance but did not fall. As I looked in the rear-view mirror I saw that he dropped the rifle. That gave me the time I needed to get away. I drove out onto the highway. We drove about three miles down the road when I saw an area with several trees. I thought we could pull in and be hidden by them. The road was a mountainous curving road and without headlights, there was too much traffic on the highway for us to be safe. We made make-shift beds in the back and the kids finally went to sleep.

Almost three hours later, my brother-in-law pulled up. He told me that Keith called him after we left and told him what he had done and asked him to go find us. He said he had been looking everywhere for us. We followed him back into town and I thought we would be safer if I could find an out-of-the-way motel. We rented a room for the night. The next morning Keith came into town and, after going to his sister's to find us, he began searching the motels in town. He finally

Chapter 13

found the car and checked in the office for our room number. He came to the room and knocked on the door. I was brushing my teeth, and one of the boys opened the door. He stormed in, slammed the door, and went past the kids just as I was racing out of the bathroom to see what was happening. He pulled his .357 magnum out of his coat pocket just enough so I could see it. He told me we had to go home and that he would follow us. We loaded up and headed out. There didn't seem to be any other choice.

When we got home, he acted as if nothing had happened. He told the kids to get ready for school, and he got dressed for work. I told him that I would drive them to school but he made them go with him. I got them in the pickup and he pulled out. I hopped in my car and followed them to make sure he took them to school. I waited for them to go into the building, and then got out and walked to each classroom to be sure that each child had made it to class. I picked them up after school and we were headed out to the car when Keith intercepted us. He told one of the boys to get in the pickup with him and he would take him home. We headed home, and things were reasonably quiet that night. The state policeman came by and sat with us for about an hour. It gave me a chance to get myself and the kids to bed. After he left, Keith fell asleep in his chair so we had a semi-quiet night.

The next weekend the kids and I planned to go out to the river and play in the water. We decided that we would drive to the gas station about three miles down the road and get some snacks and soda. We had just reached the end of the driveway when we heard a gunshot. My twelve-year-old daughter looked at me and screamed, "He's killed himself. We have to go back." I backed down the driveway, told the kids to stay in the car and ran into the house. Keith was sitting on the couch, just laughing. I could see where he had fired the gun and shattered

Chapter 13

one of the windows. I turned around, and he just kept laughing but he let me go. The children and I made another temporary escape.

Now things were happening every day. It seemed that there was no rest from the constant fear and anxiety that surrounded us. My children often lay in bed crying. I was so torn as to what I should do. I tried again to get help from my in-laws and the state policeman that came around almost nightly, but it seemed that nobody knew what to do. My father-in-law said that he could not handle Keith, and the officer said that I didn't have enough to have him arrested. He still thought that Keith's problem was alcohol. Keith was capable of acting so normal when he was at work or out in the community that my accusations seemed preposterous. All I could do was keep waiting.

Chapter 14

ಬಂಧ
*"I can do all things through Christ
which strengtheneth me."
Philippians 4:13*

Christmas came and went, and we headed into the new year. I was busy with my last semester of college. I was carrying twenty-four hours as our lives were becoming more desperate, and I knew that I had to finish as soon as I could. We had reached a point where I knew I couldn't be away from the kids. I was student teaching now at the same school my children attended and where my husband was

Chapter 14

an administrator, and I was taking three directed studies, so I did not have to make the long drive to the college every day. It was a relief for me as I was with my children now most of the time, and Keith was never alone with them.

I knew we were reaching the end of our journey. I just didn't know how it would end. Keith could barely function at home, and it was very evident that he would not be able to go on this way much longer. He was a mess emotionally, physically, and mentally. He was becoming more violent at home.

God began to work in me, preparing me for what was to come. I woke up about 4:00 one morning and sat up in bed. I looked over at Keith, and the thought came to me that I was going to be alone soon. A few days later Keith came in from work and walked over to me and kissed me hello. This was unusual and the thought came to me that he would soon be gone. Looking back, I know that God was letting me know that our lives were going to change. My waiting was coming to an end.

There were several incidences during this time when Keith became very violent. Many times the noise would wake up the children and they would come running into the room. Sometimes they jumped on him, trying to pry his hands from around my neck or pushing him away from us. He seemed to respond to their cries and would walk away.

One Sunday morning after breakfast, I was getting the kids ready for Sunday morning service. It was around 8:30. I heard Keith go out the back door. I looked out the window and he was headed for his pickup. I assumed he would drive away. But instead he got in and just sat there. He had been very quiet all morning which was unusual for him. An hour later, he was still just sitting in the pickup. He sat there all day. It was after 6:00 in the evening when he finally got out and came back into the house.

Chapter 14

As he entered our home, he brought with him such an overwhelming feeling of oppression. I could feel a heaviness pushing down on me. A greater fear than I had ever felt before came into my heart. The cloud that surrounded him was almost visible and seemed to stifle my breathing. As he walked up to me, there was a physical change in his face. His expression was lifeless and there was a leering evilness in his eyes. As I stared up at him, I had the feeling that I was looking at a stranger. This powerful sense of foreboding followed us the rest of his life. From that moment on, I lived with a stranger.

I have often pondered this time and consider it the beginning of the end. I believe that Keith spent those hours in solitude making his choice. He had two choices. He could allow God to forgive him and change his life or he could allow Satan to have the control. He could have turned to God with remorse and repentance, and God would have reached down and held him in his arms. Who knows what actually transpired during that time but when he entered the house, he did not come in alone. The fear and oppression that came with him affected all of us. Our home was no longer a safe place, and the fear was constant. The kids and I stayed outside or at school in my classroom as much as we could.

On Monday, we all went back to school and work. I was teaching, but during a break I went to the office to pick up some supplies. Keith was not in his office and I asked his secretary where he was. She told me that he had gotten sick and gone home. My first thought was that he had gone home to kill himself. I checked out of school and raced down the road to our house. When I entered the house he was in the living room watching a pornographic video. He had not openly viewed pornography, and I never came across any at home. I was unaware that this was a part of his life. I walked in and he just looked at me. I told him that he had to turn

Chapter 14

everything over to God, or he was not going to make it. He was fighting a losing battle if he continued to live the way he was. He stood up, his face twisted and contorted with such rage, as he literally shook his fist toward heaven, cursing God. It was a moment when it seemed that all sound stopped. I stood frozen where I was. I had felt the weight of oppression and fear in his presence before but this was almost unbearable. Gravity seemed to be pushing me to the floor and such a fear engulfed me that my breathing became difficult. The oppression was so stifling that all I could think about was getting out of the house. I was too afraid to turn my back to Keith so, without a word, I slowly backed out the door. I don't think he noticed that I left.

Spring break was coming up the following week, and Keith made plans to drive down south to visit an aunt and uncle who lived in a city close to the Mexican border. But on Wednesday evening, he became very ill. I think he took his bipolar medication and combined it with alcohol. He refused medical help but by early the next morning he was so ill that we had to take him to the hospital. He was in the hospital for three days. He refused to allow me to be with him when he spoke with the doctor, so I only know what he told me. At first he just said that he had an allergic reaction to the medication, but later he told me that the doctor had found cancer.

He was released from the hospital on Friday and on Saturday he wanted to leave for his aunt and uncle's house. I tried to talk him into staying home for a few days, but he was adamant about going. He promised that he would not drink. I knew that he would not keep his word. We took the camper and planned to stay for the whole week. It was with great apprehension that the kids and I got in the vehicle.

The trip was a nightmare. We did not do much of anything. We spent some time at the mall, but the rest of the week was spent sitting

Chapter 14

in a campground. The kids and I were able to get out and play in the playground, but that was about all we did. Keith became more and more out of control. He promised he wasn't drinking, but we were so afraid all of the time. He brought his .357 Magnum and just kept it on his lap everywhere we went. We never did go and visit his aunt and uncle.

On Friday morning we planned to head back home when he suddenly decided to drive across the border into Mexico. I told him that the kids and I were not going. I asked him to let us out. As we were headed toward Mexico, we had to veer into the border patrol station on the American side. Keith stopped about a fourth of a mile away and pulled over. He got out and put his gun in the camper. I followed him and told him I was going to get the kids a snack. He put up the gun and went back to the pickup. I grabbed the gun and stuffed it inside the dirty clothes hamper underneath all of the clothes. I grabbed some cookies and raced back to the cab.

We drove up to the guarded area, and the patrol officer stepped out and asked Keith why he had stopped before he drove in. I had hopes that the officer would make him get out and that Keith would be so belligerent that they would hold him. But that was not to be. He checked our IDs and looked into the camper and the pickup and waved us through.

It was sundown as we pulled back onto the highway. I knew the kids and I could not go with him any further. I told him that he needed to take us back to town and drop us off at the bus station. We were ready to go home. He argued, but I was adamant and told him that we would get out one way or the other. If he didn't take us to the bus station, we would get out at the border station. He finally whipped the pickup and camper around in the middle of the freeway. It was God's grace that we didn't have an accident.

Chapter 14

By the time we reached the bus station, the sun had already gone down and the station was closed. It was a very small building with no lights inside or out. There were two payphones hanging on the outside wall. The kids and I jumped out. I didn't have time to even grab my purse before Keith was peeling out of the drive. I headed toward the phones then realized that we had better get away while we could. I knew that Keith would soon be back looking for us. It was so unlike him to just let us go. I knew that God had given us this opportunity to escape.

I had no idea where we were. The bus station was very isolated but I could see a used car lot about half a mile down the road. I told the kids we had to get to that car lot as fast as we could and that if Dad drove up we had to just keep running. For one second, I knew that this wasn't fair for the kids, but in the next instant, I knew that made no difference. I believed we were running for our lives. We took off as fast as we could. We had just made it to the car lot when I turned around and saw Keith turning back into the bus station. I herded the kids behind and under a car and told them to stay still and not say a word. Keith drove around the bus station and got out of the pickup looking around for us. Finally he got back in the pickup and pulled back on the highway. He was driving very slowly, and I knew he was searching for us as he drove by. He passed the car lot and we gave him time to get out of sight before we again moved from car to car keeping as low as we could because we could not see which way he had driven.

We finally reached a gas station and ran in. A young man was working and there was no one else around. He was getting ready to close. I asked him if I could use the phone. The building was small, and the front of the building was solid glass. The station was very well lit. I grabbed the phone and called my in-laws collect and told them what was going on. I had $100 and my

Chapter 14

credit card in my pocket so I knew that we could get a room and get out of sight if we could just find a motel. I told them I would call them back as soon as we got a room and let them know where we were.

About that time Keith drove right up to the window. I told the young man that my husband was drunk, and we had to get away from him. I asked him to take the kids and get out of there no matter what was happening to me and then call the police. I admonished the kids to keep going even if they thought that Daddy might try to hurt me. I promised them I would be safe and would come and get them soon if they had to leave.

Keith drove up and sat staring at the window. The room was bright with lights so I know that he should have seen us. I believe that God covered his eyes and that he was not able to see that we were there. He kept looking in and looking around and then he would turn and look outside around the station. After what seemed an eternity, he drove away.

We waited for ten minutes and then headed out again. We went another mile and found a motel. We got a room and called my in-laws back. My brother-in-law said he would come and pick us up, but it would take him three to four hours. There was a fast food place nearby so we ran over and picked up some sandwiches and went back to the room. We turned on the TV and ate supper, and the kids began to relax and feel that we were safe. They were so tired, and the trauma that they had been exposed to had exhausted them. My boys were soon dozing off, but my daughter could not sleep so she and I just sat together watching silly shows. I knew that our nightmare was nearly over now. There would be no turning back this time, but I still did not know what lay ahead.

My brother-in-law showed up early the next morning, and we headed back to my in-laws

Chapter 14

home. When we arrived we found that Keith's Dad had also driven over to find Keith. The next evening he returned home and told us that he had found Keith and that they had driven back to our house and unloaded the camper. He said that Keith told him he had an administrator's meeting on Saturday, but that he would be down on Sunday, which was Easter, and would bring all the goodies for the kids. I asked him if Keith had found the gun, and he told me that he had.

I called the house during the day, but there was no answer. Keith had not mentioned an administrator's meeting to me, and I knew it was extremely unlikely that a meeting would be held on a holiday weekend. But, as I always did, I turned it over to God. It was, and had always been, out of my control. There was nothing I could do.

Finally, Keith called around 1:00 that afternoon and told me that he would bring the car to me if I would meet him in a town that was thirty-five miles away. His father and his sister decided to go with me to meet him while the kids stayed with their grandmother. He drove up at 3:00, and I could see that he was very drunk. He didn't get out of the car, but waited for us to come to him. He was upset and refused to listen as his father begged him to come back with us. He finally told me that if I would get in the car with him and drive him back home, he would let me have the car and come back.

I don't know what I was thinking, but I was reaching for the car handle when his father grabbed my arm. He told Keith that I was not going anywhere with him. I know that was God working. I believe that he planned to kill me once we were home and then take his own life. He had reached the end of his life of deceit, secrets and lies.

I don't believe that his father ever fully realized how serious Keith's problems were. He always held back, thinking that I was just exag-

Chapter 14

gerating them. God worked in him to stop me from making a terrible mistake. Keith cursed us and pulled out. Later in the evening, I tried to call him. There was no answer. I tried several times but he did not answer the phone.

Finally, with nothing left to do, we went to bed. The kids and I slept together in a twin bed. We were afraid of what had happened and what would happen. After the children finally went to sleep, I picked up a book that was on the night stand, *Angels* by Billy Graham. I was reading it when suddenly this statement jumped out at me. "In death there is perfection." I don't mean that my attention was drawn to it but it lifted right off the page and seemed to float in the air, just like in the cartoons. That was when I knew that it was over. I knew that Keith was dead.

I got up and tried to phone the house again but still no answer. I tried several times during the night and then again early morning. Finally, at 5:00 the next morning, his father got up and was making coffee. I walked in and told him that something was wrong because Keith had not answered the phone all night or this morning. He told me that after we got around we would drive up and check on him. Just as we finished talking, the phone rang. It was his work place calling him to come in to work as they had an emergency.

We didn't hear from Keith all morning and he didn't answer the phone when we called. His dad finally got home at 1:00 that afternoon. My father-in-law, my mother-in-law, my children, and I loaded up and left for our house in the mountains. We arrived a little after 3:00. As the car turned into the driveway, the house loomed into sight. It was nestled in a green valley surrounded by peaceful mountains. The quiet was deafening, and as I opened the car door I could hear the water in the nearby river gurgling as it tumbled over the rocks.

Chapter 14

At any other time, I would have paused to soak in the peacefulness of the valley but not today. The fear in my heart pushed into my chest, and my breathing became labored almost as though a heavy fog had settled in. I stepped out of the car and looked around. The yard had been cleaned and both vehicles were parked in the back yard and away from the driveway.

"Lord, I think he's finally done it. Help us." I prayed as I gathered my strength and turned to face my three children. "I want you kids to stay here in the car. I will be right back. You can't come in yet." I spoke with a quiet firmness that belied all of the thoughts and anguish going through my head.

I turned quickly and headed towards the front walk. Suddenly, my father-in-law grabbed my arm and pulled me back. He said, "I want to go in first. You stay here with the kids." With a sigh of relief, I honored his request. I knew I would eventually have to face what was inside, but I had another moment to pull myself together. I turned back and smiled at my children. This was a lot for children who were twelve, nine and eight years old to deal with and I didn't know how to make it easier for them.

Keith's father knocked on the door, but it was locked. He returned to the car and got my keys. Almost as soon as he unlocked the door and entered the house, he turned back and came rushing out.

"He's done it! He's finally done it!" He shouted, "He's killed himself."

I should have been better prepared for this moment. After all, I had expected it since our second year of marriage. But I wasn't. I looked again at my frightened children. "Remember. You stay right where you are. I will be back soon," I said as I headed for the front door. I moved as in slow motion, not wanting to face what was inside but knowing that this was what I had to do.

Chapter 14

I stepped through the door and saw my husband sitting on the couch. The television was running, but the noise faded into the background. From where I stood, the table lamp covered my view of his head. I could see that his legs were crossed and that his hands were at his side. I saw the .357 Magnum lying where it had fallen.

I paused for a moment as I again turned to God for the strength He had always provided in times of trouble. "Lord, I know that I can fall apart and not ever function again, or I can go on with my life and live the plan you have for me. Help me to do Your will." In that moment, I had a vision of my children walking around the front yard, crying. I knew that I had to go on. I had to think of my children. Even in the horror of this moment, God reminded me that I had to be there for them, to help them put the pieces of their shattered lives back together.

I stepped around the end table and saw my husband's face. I did not see a peaceful countenance, but I did see a lifeless one. And quietly I breathed, "Thank you, God. It is finally over."

At that time I did not see the horror of the scene around me. There was blood everywhere, but I was in shock and it did not register in my mind. Keith shot himself in the head with his .357 Magnum. The sheriff later told me that they were all surprised that the bullet had lodged in his brain and had not exited. It would have blown his head off. I knew that this was the grace of God once again protecting us from the horror. The scene could have been so much more violent.

The sheriff, the paramedics, and the coroner came. The sheriff took away several suicide notes, and I was never able to read them. They misplaced them and never found them. A couple of weeks later I was moving our things out when my sister came across a last note that he had written to me. He had written it on a box under our bed. I think it explained some but it would

Chapter 14

be years later before I fully understood his message. His note read, "*I love you but I hate me more.*"

We buried him in his family's plot almost exactly one week before our sixteenth wedding anniversary. His funeral was attended by people from all over the state. Students from his school were bussed in. Two pastors handled the service. I received over a hundred cards from family, friends, and acquaintances. People loved and revered him, and many hearts were saddened at his death. We were saddened with the horror, but we also rejoiced. With this loss came our freedom—freedom from violence and fear. We looked towards our chance for peace.

There was an autopsy and the report came back that he had an extremely high level of alcohol in his system. There was no cancer.

After sixteen years, I thought it was finally over. But Jesus said, "And ye shall know the truth, and the truth shall make you free" John 8:32 (KJV). I did not know the truth. I did not understand Keith's life or the great torment he struggled with. I did not understand the horror and the confusion or why he wanted to kill me. My story was not over and it would be another twenty-five years before I knew "the truth."

Chapter 15

ಸಾಧ
"And ye shall know the truth, and the
truth shall make you free."
John 8:32

We put our past behind us and moved forward. We moved in with my in-laws for a couple of months because we could not go back to the place where Keith killed himself. I took the children to counseling immediately. After several sessions, the counselor told me that they were not ready for counseling, but that they would all probably need it in the future.

I was able to transfer to another school for the remainder of my student teaching and finished my bachelor's degree in education six weeks after Keith's death. I was blessed with a job teaching at a high school that was forty miles from where my in-laws live. We moved into an apartment near the school and our new life began.

After sixteen years, I finally had such precious peace in my life. The fear of Keith coming home and drinking was gone. The fear of his out-of-control behavior was gone. I no longer worried about my husband killing us all. But there was a deep sadness in my life, too. I was sad for the loss of what I thought I had on that beautiful spring day when we promised to love and to cherish until death do us part. I was sad for the man I had married and once loved. I was sad that I had watched as Satan slowly took over his heart, mind, and body. I wondered often what had happened to all that love he had promised

Chapter 15

me. I wondered what had happened to the man I had fallen in love with. What had happened to the man I thought I had married? I still had so many questions.

God was faithful. He gave me a wonderful career as I went from teaching to administration in the public schools. I loved what I did and God provided all of the tools that I needed to be successful. He abundantly provided the finances to support my family.

The children grew up. We had our own struggles during the remainder of their growing-up years but we stayed faithful to God just as He had been so faithful to us. And I never took "that wonderful peace that passes understanding" for granted.

As the children left home, I felt more than just the sadness of the empty nest. I worried about the effect of their dysfunctional childhood and the horrors that they lived with on a daily basis. God had so greatly blessed us. All of my children had accepted Jesus Christ as Lord and Savior. They knew the Word and were faithful in church. But I also knew that our scars went deep.

I made plenty of mistakes raising these three children as a single mother but my love and devotion for them could not be questioned and I did the best I could. They were my life and I wanted each one of them to have a much better marriage relationship and future then I had. They have each had to bear their own cross. God has been gracious and, through Him, my children have broken the cycle of generational sin. They still have their issues, as I do, but God put our lives back together again.

One by one they found Christian mates, pursued education and careers, and settled down. I felt like Job in the second half of his life as God increased his blessings. Those grandchildren that I never thought I would live to see, became

Chapter 15

my reality. I retired to care for my mother who had Alzheimer's disease, and life was good.

I still thought about Keith often and sometimes pondered our life together. But my heart was no longer filled with all of the questions that I once had. They just did not seem to matter now.

But in a split second my world was turned upside down again. Twenty-five years after Keith's death, the answer to what tormented him for years came to light. I was soon to understand the moaning and wailing that rose out of his tortured soul as he fought with his demons.

Wayne and his wife came to visit. This was the same relative who had come, those many years ago, to help me when Keith was so suicidal, and the state police were called. As we were talking, I asked him if he remembered that time. I was curious about whether or not Keith had told him why he was so upset. I could sense Wayne was struggling but finally, and very quietly, he told me that Keith had told him that the night before, in his drunkenness he had raped Wayne's thirteen-year-old daughter.

My mind whirled, thinking I had missed part of the conversation and misunderstood what was said. "What did you say?" I asked. He repeated that my husband had raped his daughter when she was thirteen years old. He first thought that Keith made up the story because he was just trying to anger him. He thought Keith believed that if Wayne was angry enough he might shoot him and help him commit suicide. He never dreamed it could be true so he did not ask his daughter. Several years after Keith's death, when his daughter was in college, she told him that Keith had indeed raped her that night.

My mind shut down. I couldn't respond. My head was buzzing, and I was engulfed in pain as I tried to sort through the thoughts that were racing through my mind. How could I conceivably absorb the news I had just heard? How

Chapter 15

---

was this possible? How could I have been so deceived? I had lived through so much abuse and even twenty-five years after his death he was still able to reduce me to such a helpless state.

The silence was broken. "I thought you knew," he said.

"How could I have known?" I asked him. My voice was barely audible. I forced myself to get up and I walked out the door.

As God has always worked in my life, He immediately provided a place and a godly man to help me understand and begin to process what I had just heard. I had been seeing a counselor for a couple of months because I was having some problems with anxiety and was worried that I needed to deal with my past. As I stepped outside, God reminded me that I had an appointment scheduled with my counselor for that morning and had only twenty minutes to get there. Up until that moment, I had been so busy with my company that I had completely forgotten about it. In His mercy and grace, I was able to deal with this situation immediately. God did not give me the chance to push this news back and hide from it. He provided the resources I needed to begin working through my pain within an hour of the news.

There was never a moment that I doubted what Wayne said. I knew it was true. It all made sense. I suddenly began to understand Keith's behavior on the day following the rape. He was fearful that she would tell and that he would end up in prison. He knew he had allowed his sexual perversion to hit too close to home. He had gone into a drunken rage, and that was when I had to call for help.

As I began to make the connection with his behavior after the rape, memories began pouring through my mind. Just like a computer has pop-up messages, I could see events and words from my life running before my eyes. I

Chapter 15

realized that the first time my husband tried to shoot me, when I was pregnant with our first child, had been the first time he had a sexual affair. The memories just kept flying through my mind. I remembered that Keith had told me that this same thirteen-year-old girl had been raped by an uncle on her mother's side. I told him that if it were my daughter, I would have killed him. I now realize that he was trying to see my reaction to know if Wayne had told me anything.

Another time I was commenting on how great our community was, and he told me that I didn't know all that went on. He informed me that a father of three of the high school girls where he worked would prostitute them out. I told him that if he knew it was true, he had to report it. But now I realize, he knew because he was probably paying for their services.

So many more comments that he made to me now connected with different events in our lives. I do not know how many affairs, rapes, and sexual encounters he had over the years, but I am greatly saddened for those he hurt. I do know that a pedophile rapes over and over. There were many instances when he mysteriously disappeared from home, from work and from vacations.

He was so tormented by his double life that his only hope was to kill us both so that I would never find out. God never allowed him to pull that trigger. Keith struggled with his own death because he knew that he would have to face God and every time he tried to end it he just couldn't do it. Those moans and groans that came from so deeply inside of him came from the guilt and horror at what his life had become. And I know, without a doubt, that God miraculously intervened and kept him from ending my life and protected my children.

For all of our years together, he was leading a double life. In the daylight, he was a fine, upstanding, church-going member of the com-

Chapter 15

munity but in the dark he was a pedophile, rapist, adulterer, and only God knows what else. I trusted him. I struggle with the fact that he worked with teenagers and I am sure that he took advantage of many young girls over the years.

I knew he had betrayed me in so many ways but I never once suspected him of adultery. I have had to face the reality that he never loved me but just saw me as a good, moral Christian girl—the kind of girl he was supposed to marry. After we married, I learned how wild he had been. He allowed Satan a stronghold in his life when he was young, and he never asked God to free him. His bondage continued until his death.

My first reaction was to take my "Taurus 40" and go to the cemetery and shoot holes through his grave and into his coffin. I had a lot to work through! But the first thing I actually did was call and talk with my children about it. I had to assure myself that he never molested my children and

I wanted them to hear the truth from me. Even in my brokenness, they were supportive and helped me know that I could get through this.

I know that there are people out there who knew about his indiscretions. There were those who were his victims. But nobody told. Nobody spoke up. By their silence he was empowered to hurt others. And for some reason God kept the truth from me until decades had passed.

I am thankful that I finally know the truth. I do not understand his actions any more than before I knew his "secrets." But with God's grace, I have been able to forgive Keith, and I have found closure to that part of my life. The truth has set me free, and I am free indeed. God is faithful.

CPSIA information can be obtained at www.ICGtesting.com
Printed in the USA
LVOW132157250113

317341LV00001B/1/P